Normandy Invasion
D-Day and the Path to Victory

Normandy Invasion
D-Day and the Path to Victory

By

Frederick Hastings

Vij Books
New Delhi (India)

Published by

Vij Books
(*An Imprint of Vij Books India Pvt Ltd*)
(Publishers, Distributors & Importers)
4836/24, 3rd Floor, Ansari Road
Delhi – 110 002
Phone: 91-11-43596460
Mobile: 98110 94883
e-mail: contact@vijpublishing.com
www.vijbooks.in

Copyright © 2024

ISBN: 978-81-19438-57-0 (PB)

All rights reserved.

Contents

1	**Planning the Invasion: Operation Overlord**	1
	• The Strategic Vision	1
	• The Veil of Secrecy: Intelligence and Deception in Operation Overlord	5
	• Logistical Challenges	8
	• Unity in Diversity: Coordinating the Allied Forces in Operation Overlord	12
	• Precision and Prudence: The Final Preparations for D-Day	15
2	**The Airborne Assault: Pathfinders and Paratroopers**	19
	• The Strategic Role of Airborne Forces in Operation Overlord	19
	• Trailblazers of the Skies: The Pathfinders of D-Day	23
	• From the Sky to the Battlefield: The Paratrooper Landings of D-Day	27
	• Silent Wings: The Glider Operations of D-Day	31
	• Shielding the Beaches: The Tactical Role of Securing the Flanks in D-Day Operations	34

3	**The Beach Landings: Sword, Juno, Gold, Omaha, and Utah**	38
	• The First Step to Caen: The Assault on Sword Beach	38
	• Triumph at Juno Beach: The Canadian Contribution to D-Day	42
	• Securing Gold Beach: The British Triumph on D-Day	46
	• Blood and Sand: The Battle for Omaha Beach	50
	• The Western Vanguard: Utah Beach and the Triumph of the 4th Infantry Division	54
4	**Breaking Through: Allied Advances Inland**	58
	• Beyond the Beaches: The Allies' Initial Breakout Efforts in Normandy	58
	• The Battle of the Bocage: Navigating Normandy's Natural Fortress	63
	• Operation Cobra: The Breakout from Normandy	67
	• Allied Coordination and Challenges in Normandy	71
	• Turning the Tide: The Liberation of Key Towns in Normandy	75
5	**The Push to Victory: Liberation of France**	79
	• Encircling Triumph: The Battle of the Falaise Pocket	79

- The Liberation of Paris: A Triumph of Allied Forces and French Resistance   83
- Across the Fields of Liberation: Allied Advances Through France   87
- Sustaining Victory: The Logistical and Strategic Challenges of the Allied Advance   90
- The Final Thrust: Allies' Road to Germany   94

Appendix   99

Key Commanders in the Allied Advance Across France and Into Germany   99

- General Dwight D. Eisenhower   99
- Field Marshal Bernard Montgomery   99
- General Omar Bradley   99
- General George S. Patton   100
- General Charles de Gaulle   100
- General Harry Crerar   100
- General Philippe Leclerc   101

1

Planning the Invasion: Operation Overlord

The Strategic Vision

Operation Overlord remains a watershed point in World War II; it was the beginning of an unyielding campaign that finally resulted in the end of Nazi Germany. The strategic conception behind this docket giant was not just that of effecting an invasion but of carefully planning a multi-dimensional operation that ensured a lasting foothold in Western Europe was realised. Crafted by some of the most brilliant military minds of the time, this audacious plan aimed to fracture formidable German defences and set the stage for the liberation of occupied territories, thus altering the course of the war.

Operation Overlord was of such paramount importance. By mid-1944, Axis powers, despite the setbacks on the Eastern Front and in North Africa, still found them to be credible adversaries. The German war machine was thus scattered throughout the continent, backed by this series of outgrowths, which formed what has since come to be known as the 'Atlantic Wall'. As the Allies knew, an invasion of Western Europe had to relieve the pressure on Soviet forces in the east by liberating occupied territories and had to prepare the ground for an attack to rip the Nazi regime from its foundations. Hence, the strategic vision of Operation Overlord arose: the need to create a firm and lasting foothold in France through which a comprehensive Allied drive into the German heartland could then come.

So many famous leaders were heading the combined massive effort who made this plan possible. The other day, General Dwight D. Eisenhower was made Supreme Commander of the Allied Expeditionary Force, and he was to take the helm in leading the allies in the invasion. Leadership under Eisenhower's guidance was comprised of his leadership in bringing out the spirit of cooperation in these very diverse forces. British, American, Canadian, and other troops had one goal and were moving together. Indeed, the strategic acumen of this great man and his delicate diplomatic touch were critical in uniting, harmonising, and balancing the often conflicting interests and strategies of the various Allied nations.

Another great man associated with the planning and execution of Operation Overlord was General Bernard Montgomery; he commanded the ground invasion during its initial stages. The comprehensiveness of Montgomery's effort in detailing everything to the point of defeating any unforeseen hindrance is the reason the whole success of the landing is attributed to him and his seriousness in landing. He had, of course, learned the lessons from the problems entailed in great amphibious operations during previous campaigns, like the battles in the desert of North Africa. Montgomery, of course, was looking very far ahead, past the lodgment problem, during his planning period toward the campaigning that would of necessity, follow the breakout from the Normandy beachhead to develop during the advances to percolate deeply into France.

Of course, there was a host of important leaders and planners besides Eisenhower and Montgomery. Admiral Sir Bertram Ramsay led the naval aspects of the invasion and arranged the massive armada needed in facilitating the landing and reaching the English Channel for the Allied troops. His naval warfare expertise and experience in the evacuation of Dunkirk, in hindsight, were invaluable. The operation was led by Air Chief Marshal Sir Trafford Leigh-Mallory, who saw to it that the crucial requirement of winning of air superiority was done by the Allies—the same was a prerequisite for the success of protecting the invasion and for the hindrance of the German reinforcement.

It would be all-comprehensive planning for Operation Overlord, later to be rated by many as the master's class in strategic operations, and inherent in the planned operation were phases calculated to expose to chance those waves of success in the concomitant minimisation of the risk. The opposition to this front, meanwhile, comprised amphibious landings that the troops made on five beachheads across the Normandy coast, which bore their respective codename: Sword, Juno, Gold, Omaha, and Utah. These beaches are distributed over the various Allied forces of the army. The British and Canadians opposed Sword, Juno, and Gold, while the Americans were set up against the beachheads of Omaha and Utah. This dispersion of forces was thus designed to paralyse German defences with overwhelming force and allow the establishment of a series of beachheads that could then be tactically be linked to one another as a continuous front.

Fundamental to this strategy was the achievement of air and naval superiority. The Allies knew that control in the air and at sea was to be achieved in whatever force necessary to cover the assault of these invading forces and to protect the battle line from any German reinforcement. In the months leading up to the invasion, the allies had a series of large-spread bombings of German railways, bridges, and airfields. This coupled with an ongoing air patrol and naval blockade worked well to disable the German capacity to effectively respond in a timely manner.

The remaining elements of the strategy were meant to capitalise on the earlier stages of success the beach landings would offer. After the beachheads had been secured, the plan then entailed rapid enlargement of the bridgehead, interlocking of the separate landing zones to effect one united front, followed by the securing of some key towns and villages, establishment of supplies then preparation of defensible positions for further projected offensives. The final aim was to break through the German defensive lines in order to open the way into Paris, liberate the French capital in order to inflict a psychological and strategic defeat on the Nazi regime.

Deception and surprise played a very important part in this plan. Operation Fortitude, a plan under which the Allied forces caused complete confusion regarding the place of landing, played an important part. By creating the illusion of an assault on the Pas de Calais, the Allies diverted crucial German forces from Normandy, diminishing the strength of the defenses that the attacking units would have to encounter.

In the larger historical point, Operation Overlord changed the course of events. The assaults, combined with those in Normandy, marked the Chrisindlerinee-beginning downfall of Nazi Germany. With a firm Allied presence established in Western Europe, further things could be said: the liberation of a number of occupied countries, the inflating of the morale that was badly needed for the nations of the Allies, and the forcing of Germans to fight a war on multiple theaters from multiple fronts. That which was built from the campaign's momentum in Normandy carried through to the liberation of Paris and beyond, right on to the destruction of Germany in May 1945.

On reflection, the intention of strategy lying behind Operation Overlord proves to be witness of the acuteness, pluck, and of the collaborative instinct characterised into the Allied. It was such an eventful and well-devised plan, taking leaps of boldness with precision planning and balancing each strength of the allies' nations at the hands of their military heads. Successful execution of Operation Overlord will not only change the outcomes of World War II but also send the prospect immediately into the rebuilding from post-war in Europe and finally to lasting peace.

The Veil of Secrecy: Intelligence and Deception in Operation Overlord

Operation Overlord—its very success hung on subtleties of intelligence and deception—in addition to the tremendous force already pronounced. This information was critical to the clandestine efforts that were to be made to discern critical puzzles of the German defence puzzle and would be pivotal in misleading the enemy about the actual site of the invasion. The frantically important work behind this game of double agents and counterintelligence was undertaken by British MI6, American OSS, and the French Resistance, even as ariel and sea reconnaissance runs provided the Allies with the detailed intelligence that would ensure the daring plan had no real chance to prosper. At the core of this operation was Operation Fortitude, a mastermind deception that led German eyes and ears far afield from the beaches of Normandy, allowing confusion and mistrust within the enemy's decision-making process.

The influence of espionage within the web of intelligence for Operation Overlord was indeed far-reaching and intricate. British MI6 was experienced in such analyses and initiated a network of spies and informers all over occupied Europe. What they did was put their lives on the line to infiltrate German military installations, seek details on the movements of the troops, and report back on the strength and disposition of enemy forces. The intelligence with which MI6 emerged had played a critical role in pointing out weak spots in the German defenses extending along the Normandy coast, as well as reflecting the generalised strategic landscape of the opposition to be faced by the Allies.

Running with a similar mandate but some activities parallel to MI6, the OSS had been operating. The OSS, as the forerunner to the CIA of today, was engaged in several racially diverse intelligence, sabotage, and recruitment—not to forget local informants. It has always worked hand in glove with the MI6, holding common interests and activities that shall bolster their work, each learning from one another in the process. Indeed, this transatlantic cooperation reflected the unity of purpose that characterised the Allied war effort.

Of equal importance, however, to the successful workings of that intelligence were the activities of the French Resistance. Operating as an organisation created from disparate individuals against German occupation, the Resistance offered crucial support regarding local information and aid. Participants undertook sabotage, disturbed German supply lines, and gathered minute detail on enemy fortifications. Their detailed information regarding the local ground conditions or facilities proved invaluable to the Alliance's planning. It is impossible to exaggerate the sheer courage and determination of the men of the Resistance; their work had an impact not only in terms of supplying the necessary raw data to the Allied intelligence machine but even to such lengths that were utilised to improve the general efficiency of the Alliance intelligence system.

Although human intelligence was the integral product of espionage, observation thoroughly gave a broad overview of theaters of operation in the air and the sea. The aerial reconnaissance—the systematic photographing of German emplacements along the French coast by the Royal Air Force and the United States Army Air Forces—also entailed dangers, including compulsory high-resolution photographs taken at great perils for the pilots in such sorties, accompanied by much thoughtful study on the part of intelligence officers. Such photographs were invaluable as they exposed the layout of beach defenses and the positioning of gun batteries, as well as the construction of beach obstacles designed to repulse an amphibious assault. With this type of information available, it was possible to provide detailed maps and models of the cross-channel invasion beaches for the Allied powers' planners. It was, therefore, put into action to ensure that the assault forces were well rehearsed beforehand with a full view of the challenge that lay ahead of them.

Information gathered from naval reconnaissance would add to this with an insight into the German coastal defenses. He also stated that submarines and different types of small boats performed clandestine operations near the shore of enemy areas to gather intelligence on various types of water obstructions, including enemy patrol movements. Paramount to he said the unpredictable dangers of these operations as the patrols groups reach the range of the German coastal guns and patrol boats. Yet, ruefully, this type of intelligence gleaned from these operations was at the core and of fundamental worth to the amphibious landings and of free, safe passage of the ships to the wartime invasion.

Perhaps the crowning achievement of the Allied intelligence efforts was Operation Fortitude, the most ambitious and intricate deception campaign ever produced. The whole point was to mislead the German High Command on the actual place and time of the awaited Allied landing. So this particular operation would be broken down into two suboperations: Fortitude North, cross-examined for the middling of the invasion in Norway, and then the south would turn its sights on the Pas de Calais as being the most likely place of the invasion. In particular, Fortitude South was of special importance for it to achieve its goal of steering away from Normandy and holding the German concentrations of troops away from the Pas de Calais so it would ultimately achieve the goal set:. This was partly managed by faking radio traffic, setting up dummy formations for military units, and by double agents in the German Intelligence Service passing on false intelligence. One such Havrincourt double agent was the spy from Spain, Juan Pujol García. He operated under a cover name 'Garbo' and, with his set of fictional sub-agents, provided the Germans with a plethora of misinformation. The dummy tanks and aircraft with landing craft were in complete decoration toward the illusion of the significant build-up in southeastern England. As such, these inflatables were thus put on imposition: strategic locations and optimal positioning, all to appear regarding the most enormous force of invasion ready to turn up against the Pas de Calais. So successful was this deception caper that as soon as landings at Normandy started, the Germans still held to their thinking that the actual main invasion was still to come, probably coming at Pas de Calais. They procrastinated on strengthening their reinforcements from Pass de Calais to Normandy until it was too late.

Operation Fortitude worked successfully because the deception had been carefully worked out and planned down to the last detail by the Allies. By being deceptive, one of several possible misleading truths was exposed while another was pursued actively—it completely surprised the Germans strategically, drastically lessening the potential German response and defense against Allied landings in Normandy. That grain of surprise, married to comprehensive intelligence drawn from espionage and reconnaissance, was vital to winning the beachheads and establishing a toehold in Western Europe.

Now, the collection of intelligence for Operation Overlord involved all the most secret yet highly innovative assets in aerial and marine reconnaissance; because these efforts linked together perfectly with brilliant Operation Fortitude, webs of deception were laid that would lead to the entrapment of the German high command and consequently allow of the liberation of Europe by the Allies. To date, all these lessons learned from intelligence operations continue to find their uses in developing a military strategy. This tends to imply that information and deception will forever form a critical aspect of conducting war.

Logistical Challenges

As gargantuan as the strategic vision associated with Overlord were its logistic difficulties. These critical parts underlaid the success of the D-Day invasion: a small wonder it worked, with the massive magnitude effort behind it, rigorous training regimens for the troops, and ingenious innovative infrastructural development. The relentless pursuit of victory by the Allied, with unrivaled logistical ingenuity and system coordination, left no other doorstep for the logisticians of war's logistics landscape to change.

No known operation in history had such enormous significant massive resource allocation like in Operation Overlord. These resources involved are countless, be it troops, vehicles, weapons, and supplies, besides others. Over 156,000 soldiers were used on D-Day, more than 5,000 ships and landing craft, more than 11,000 aircraft, and many of them with tanks, trucks, and other vehicles. Hence, there is a need for proper planning and coordination to make full-scale mobilisation successful in involving as many of the Allied nations as possible to accomplish the operation. Although each contingent brought to the task at hand its particular strengths, the logistics of getting together and integrating these disparate forces into a coherent invasion force proved to be nothing less than Herculean.

Feats of logistics achieved in the run-up to D-Day involved huge stockpiling of ammunition, fuel, medical supplies, and rations. These had to be pooled in significant quantities in southern England, ready to move forward at any moment. Thereby, it meant that the loading of the required resources and the dispensation of these resources were vital to its sustenance. The Allies had to keep a steady line of supplies across the Channel. This demanded great logistical networks that could be as dynamic in figurative context as the battlefront situation that prevailed.

Training and preparation formed an integral part of the Operation Overlord. They received intensive training that would emulate the amphibious assaults and the ghostly combat situations that they were to face in Normandy. This kind of training prepared the soldiers for amphibious assault techniques, where they were trained to disembark from the ships and move through the dangerous waters to access the beaches. This kind of preparation entailed a unique operation that saw the development of the particular apparatuses used in the amphibious assault, such as the Higgins boats. Such vessels, with their shallow draughts and front ramps, were designed to land troops and vehicles directly on the beaches through natural and artificial obstructions.

Second in terms of novelty was the establishment of the Mulberry harbors. Artificial harbors were constructed for the rapid off-loading of cargo onto the invasion beaches without competing with and using established ports, which the Germans heavily fortified. The Mulberry harbors were giant floating roadways and piers towed across the Channel and pieced together off the coast of Normandy. With their emplacement, the Allies had made it able to keep lymph fluids and supplies, as well as reinforcements, which poured ashore, building on the momentum of the invasion.

Coordination of air and naval support was a subject of further training. The pilots and airmen were intensively taught about bombing, strafing, and close air support for the troops on the land. At the same time, naval crews rehearsed the complex maneuvers involved in placing landing craft squarely on their beaches and delivering maritime gunfire. Thus, joint actions at sea, in the air, and on land went off like clockwork thanks to comprehensive training programs.

The infrastructure building played a lead role in emerging from the logistical issues of Operation Overlord. The Mulberry Harbours are rated number two on the list of outstanding military engineering achievements. These temporary arrears—built and off-loaded—enabled thousands of tons a day of supplies off-loaded by the Allies in ports that were otherwise practically nonexistent in the opening weeks of the invasion. These harbors presented a considerable challenge of engineering feat and planning. The unit assembly rendered each harbor made up of floating breakwaters, piers, and roadways, constructed on location and masterminded to withstand the rigors of the Channel.

Building the supply lines across the English Channel was another crucial part of the log operation. The creation resulted in a supply chain that could optimally respond bend to the fluctuating needs of the invasion force in reaching optimised positions. This system consisted not just of vessels and landing craft but also of pipelines laid underwater—known as PLUTO, Pipeline Under The Ocean—through which fuel could be conducted from England to the various points of battles in France. These pipelines under the water were quite an accomplishment. They delivered a steady stream of fuel desperately needed for the many vehicles and equipment so central to the conduct of the war.

But having done all these logistical gymnastics simply to provide all the supplies essential to help in the invasion, They also had to cater to the long-term needs of the campaign and be able to continue supporting their forces as they advanced into France and toward Germany. All this involved forward supply depots working on equipment and the medical care of the wounded. Logistical planners had to cater to every contingency: replace lost or damaged equipment, and evacuated casualties quickly.

An integrated command structure was crucial for coordination among the branches of the military and many different Allied nations from three continents. That entailed communication and a unified command. The Supreme Headquarters Allied Expeditionary Force, under its Supreme Commander General Dwight D. Eisenhower, coordinated the entire kin and held ultimate responsibility for ensuring that logistical efforts were in synchrony and running smoothly.

She judged testimony of the slowing down of the logging nuclear success of Operation Overlord, venture, energy, and a cooperative effort reaching across the board, not only of the Allies. The careful distribution of resources, thorough training, final preparation of troops, and innovative works in infrastructure were critically important in helping the Allies break into the fortification of the Atlantic Wall, gain a foothold on the Normandy beaches, and put in place all prerequisites for the subsequent liberation of Western Europe and, eventually, the defeat of Nazi Germany. Finally, the logistics caught up with the strategic scenario of Operation

Overlord; the lessons from it guide military strategy and planning even today. This shows that as long as war is prosecuted, logistics will always remain relevant to its conduct.

Unity in Diversity: Coordinating the Allied Forces in Operation Overlord

Operation Overlord, the invasion of Normandy by the allied forces, was not only powerful military action but also required combining and coordinating a multi-nation that had soldiers from United States of America, Britain, Canada and other allied countries. In this case, people needed to work together in ways that had never been seen before because there were many different languages spoken among them; they needed to understand each other's military tactics which were also dissimilar at times due to their own national interests conflicting with those of others around them etcetera this being done may seem impossible however it was achieved through establishments like Supreme Headquarters Allied Expeditionary Force (SHAEF) whose responsibility was to provide necessary channels through which orders would flow from one point down all levels until they reach those who execute them thus making sure no man acted alone but rather as part of a bigger picture always.

Bringing together varying military tactics among nations was challenging. Every country had something unique about how they do their things operationally but this was not meant to be a strength since it created a challenge for other countries. For example, America's vast industrial capacity helped produce a lot materials and manpower while Britain's long period in wars made it possible them gain experience in strategic planning however Canada among other states like Australia New Zealand or some European exiles also had specific roles since they provided soldiers as well as specialised units too although these were just among others which means that there were many more pieces of such kind whose integration demanded careful consideration along with flexibility so that there may be unity without uniformity.

The issues of international force assimilation were numerous. Language disparities in addition to different military vocabularies could result in misinterpretations which called for explicit communication protocols establishment. For the allied forces to succeed there had to be training drills and combined operations. These drills carried out in months preceding the invasion helped to streamline methods of operating and enable units from different countries to work together without any difficulties Units from different countries could not have worked together effectively had it not been these exercises which were used standardise procedures . The idea was to create trust and interoperability among the allies so that they could act as one despite their diverse backgrounds.

The center for organising all these activities lay with setting up Supreme Headquarters Allied Expeditionary Force (SHAEF) . It was at SHAEF where all plans about Overlord were being made and implemented too. Controlled by General Dwight D. Eisenhower, it was the main organ that had been given the responsibility to see into it that different nationalities fought under a single leadership. Eisenhower's ability to lead despite of having nations with opposing strategies and views was key. His diplomatic skills were what kept peace among leaders from different countries which had different beliefs thus making them achieve common goals

Command structures within SHAFF were organised in such a way as to bring out the best from each leader together with their country's strengths. The task of being in charge ground troops during D-Day landings up to when they would have made bridges across waterways behind enemy lines went to General Bernard Montgomery who was an experienced British commander. Creation these bridges was also among other things that Montgomery had been told do like ensuring thorough preparations besides his detailed plans among others primarily contributed towards success during initial attack On naval matters however everything fell under Admiral Sir Bertram Ramsay a notable officer in the British navy. He therefore coordinated various vessels used for this purpose ensuring that soldiers reached safely even though it meant some swimming for short distances because boats could not go beyond certain points due shallow waters.

The air component of the operation was under the command of Air Chief Marshal Sir Trafford Leigh-Mallory. His task was to achieve and maintain air superiority, protecting the invasion forces from German air attacks and providing crucial support to the ground operations. The coordinated efforts of these commanders, under the overarching leadership of Eisenhower, exemplified the collaborative spirit that was essential to the success of Operation Overlord.

Despite the concerted efforts to foster unity, strategic disagreements among the Allies were inevitable. These disagreements often stemmed from differing national priorities and military philosophies. One notable example was the debate over the timing and location of the invasion. Some British leaders, including Prime Minister Winston Churchill, initially favoured a strategy of peripheral attacks and operations in the Mediterranean, rather than a direct assault on the heavily fortified French coast. This approach was seen as a way to weaken Germany gradually. However, the American leadership, including General Eisenhower, advocated for a decisive invasion of Western Europe, believing it was the most direct path to victory.

Resolving such disagreements required diplomacy and a willingness to compromise. Eisenhower's role as the supreme commander was pivotal in navigating these tensions. He emphasised the importance of a unified strategy and worked tirelessly to reconcile differing viewpoints. Through a combination of persuasive argumentation and strategic concessions, Eisenhower managed to secure broad agreement on the overall plan for Operation Overlord. The eventual consensus on the Normandy invasion as the focal point of the Allied effort was a testament to the effectiveness of this collaborative approach.

The appropriation of resources and the prioritisation of different war fronts was another area where the Allies often disagreed. The British, who had many colonies to protect, feared spreading themselves too thin. Meanwhile, America's abundance of resources meant that they could afford to be more aggressive and far-reaching. For the allies to present a united front, it was necessary to reconcile these conflicting views through diplomacy. Therefore all sides had to make concessions and adjust their strategic objectives accordingly in light of this fact.

The success of Operation Overlord lay not only in careful military planning but also in political diplomacy among nations.

The success of the invasion depended on the ability to combine and control multinational forces with different national objectives, resolve differences in strategy and remain jointly against common enemies. These are still relevant lessons learnt in modern warfare showing that unity is strength therefore parties involved must communicate, have shared objectives and be ready for compromise.

Operation Overlord's coordination logistically and strategically tells volumes about combined resolve as well as ingenuity of allied powers It further emphasises significance effective leadership coupled with cooperation when dealing with challenges that are involved in running multinational military operations Collective will power among nations was tested during this period and it proved beyond any reasonable doubts that where there is a will there certainly is a way.

Precision and Prudence: The Final Preparations for D-Day

Getting ready for Operation Overlord the landing of allied forces on Normandy in 1944 is a good example of both thorough planning and looking ahead. Deciding when the invasion was supposed to be, changing it slightly, raising soldiers spirit and very strict safety measures were important and they needed to be done precisely. Each action taken during these final weeks shows how much attention to detail there was on behalf of all participants from beginning to end; nothing had been left out which might help towards the success of what had come be known as one most ambitious military undertakings ever attempted by man.

It was necessary to choose the day that would be best for such an important event considering different conditions had to be met at once. The most significant ones were connected with tides, moonlight and weather forecast among others; everything had come together in this decision. For instance, there had to be a full moon so as not only lighten up areas where planes carrying paratroopers flew but also make sure these soldiers saw their way clear once they landed; it also had be low tide by morning break because if that did not happen then all beaches would still remain covered with water while enemy could easily shoot them from higher ground.

After talking over matters thoroughly with his generals and meteorologists General Dwight D. Eisenhower decided on 5th June 1944 as an initial date having met each of these requirements. However, this day's weather forecast predicted strong storms which posed serious threat to success rates expected during such landings if they were attempted under their conditions. Thus it became necessary for him postpone decision making by twenty-four hours moving invasion day forward one more day June 6th when conditions appeared more favourable although chance something going wrong due atmospheric instability still existed within margins allowed any operation under such circumstances.

In the interval before the attack, final changes were made at the eleventh hour in the light of the newest intelligence and reconnaissance reports. Updated information on German defences, troop movements and beach defences would be sought through the last series of reconnaissance flights. This information had to be collected quickly into the invasion plan so that the units carrying out this work were being given their final instructions.

Aerial photography made known the extent of beach obstacles and minefields thus requiring changes in landing zones plus arrangements for special engineering brigades to clear such obstructions.

Together with speeches, different mental preparations were made to build up the soldiers' morale. This involved giving them motivation materials like letters from home, photographs, and propaganda leaflets showing the crimes committed by the Nazis as well as stressing on their duty to liberate occupied Europe. These efforts were meant to create among soldiers a sense of worthiness and friendship so that they could be ready psychologically for what lay ahead.

The significance of observing very tight security measures aimed at preventing any information leaks regarding the invasion plan cannot be overemphasised. The element of surprise was vital in the success of Operation Overlord and any security breach would have had very fatal outcomes. Consequently, rigorous censorship and counter-espionage tactics were put in place by the allies. Communication lines were highly controlled while everything concerning the invasion was made top secret.

Troops and equipment were moved secretly with units only being briefed about their specific duties at the eleventh hour. Information flow was based on need-to-know hence details were compartmentalised thus reducing chances of disclosure. In addition, more efforts were directed towards counter-espionage activities in a bid to identify and deal with potential threats from enemy agents. Furthermore, there existed an elaborate misinformation scheme known as "Operation Fortitude" whose main objective was to deceive the Germans about actual place and time for landing in Normandy. Double agents, fake radio communications as well as dummy installations were used under this plan so as to make enemy believe that an attack on Pas de Calais is imminent rather than that of Normandy.

Any single one of us could have landed and been back at home in three weeks. Never is one's mind more active than up to the last moment before an operation. Here are the young soldiers who actually come across reality on the internet. Last night a tremendous air battle was going on over our heads and guns were thundering from the coast as though a heavy bombardment was in progress, so either the invasion is on or else there is a great aerial fight taking place. My present mood is physically sleepy, mentally wide awake against the present company (Time to sleep!!!) . A letter has just come from Churchill which I must show to Monty— no doubt he will tear it up—in which Winston gives the date of D Day as today. Our hearts and hopes go out to them. They have waited for long years for landings, and they have never failed to do their utmost when it has fallen to them; but now, after years of preparation, the hour has struck and the time has come. I hope to hear of a particular person being caught; I have information about him, unfortunately he was not found till after the crash which killed him, and the papers which would have established his identity were all burned. I trust that those concerned will not mistake the intention which caused me to veil certain date[347]. It all sounds very much like it might be livened up soon! At that time of night one can see every star that there is in the sky. I should say that during the last four or five days there has been a great deal more air activity in this country than I have been used to; so the less noise we make to-night the better.

2

The Airborne Assault: Pathfinders and Paratroopers

The Strategic Role of Airborne Forces in Operation Overlord

One of the primary strategic moves that led to the success of Normandy's Allied invasion was the invasion of the airborne forces. They were capable of interfering with the defenses of the Germans, capturing the critical positions, and made the way for the sea-based force through the interrupted way. Leaving the sky and falling behind the enemy sector was the style chosen by them to put disorder and demolition among the German forces - and it was these means that managed to enable the vehicles that landed on the beaches. The meticulousness in the strategic planning, and the high level of skill performed in achieving their missions were the outstanding character traits that characterised the entire Normandy Campaign of the Allies.

It is beyond any doubt that in Operation Overlord the airborne forces were called upon to play the role of the catalysts in a variety of ways. The suitably designed division was to be the tip of the spear in the attack, hitting the crucial lines before the force of the sea began. The mission of airborne forces was primarily to disturb the German lines of defense leading to the victory of the seaborne attacks on the beaches. The parachutists aimed to take the Germans by surprise when jumping in the back of the Atlantic Wall. Actually, they wanted to grab important sites, such as bridges and streets, in the case of that blocking the Germans' route in Office and trapping the United States' incursion there as the only solution. This approach was intended to confuse the Germans, forcing them to split their forces and have to deal with a rear defense line as well as a facing one.

The contribution of the airborne units was critical in the general game of invasion. They would capture and secure vital bridges that are the main transportation route of troops and equipment to maintain the movement of the operation. The airborne personnel made sure the allies could cross rivers and canals and bypass the German armies at high speed and without any delay. They carried out the additional assignment of taking major roads also to assist in the quick march of the seaborne forces and interrupt the German logistics and communications. These activities were structured in such a manner that when the first parachute troops started taking the German lines, the overall action would be a long string of positive results for the Allied cambistries.

Creating disorder and confusion among the German defenders' ranks was the second highly important task. The unexpected arrival of airborne troops behind enemy lines was made to destroy the German command by forcing them to expand the resources towards the other areas to deal with the new threat. This action was also supported by the surprise element. The strategic countermeasure stressed the prevailing defects in the military condition of German. Attacking from unexpected directions and focusing on the crucial areas of the German defensive network, the airborne forces can create a situation of chaos and disorganisation, which means it will be a lot harder for Germany to defend the invasion as a whole.

The nature of the airborne units and the quality of the training aimed to underscore their unique role in Operation Overlord. The 82nd and 101st U.S. Airborne Divisions, in cooperation with the British 6th Airborne Division, were the main force deployed in the airborne assault. These divisions recruited soldiers who had undergone a thorough and rigorous military training, chosen for their endurance, courage, and capability to cope amidst external challenges autonomously. The units instruction was comprehensive and stringent, and it consisted of a wide variety of tactics and skills that were essential for airborne operations execution.

Parachute delivery is a major aspect of the training, the soldiers undergo an extended practice of the leaving the aircraft. They also learn the procedures for safe exit, and landing on different terrains. Training on how to conduct night jumps was, of course, carried out and the activity was the hardest for those involved; its severity was due to the need for minute precision and coordination between the soldiers and pilots. The troops' heightened performance of executing a precise landing in the pre-determined dropping zones was crucial for mission success, as they could scatter landings, low cover and defence could result if the landings were haphazard.

In addition to the previously mentioned elements, learning the elements and tactics of combat used by the soldiers is another necessary part of the training. They are trained to use firearms, hand-to-hand techniques, and small fighting units, which enabled them to interact with and kill the enemy. Exercises in such an environment were mostly about handling the situation and introducing the tactic of defense. The airborne troops would rarely have landed on the ground, moving between various sites with varying weather conditions. Their devices would be used for narrowcasting and other devices would be for relaying crucial communication links with the aviation unit.

Working with other Allied forces was another important part of the training. The seaborne invasion forces were only able to work with the paratroopers in a particular way of making them synchronise and co-operate on board the ships, on the beaches and during the battle. This synchronicity comprised practicing joint exercise with parachuting and water-warfare troops, where the different units practiced carrying out the respective responsibilities while they developed the communication procedures that would enable them to work together effectively. The combination of these elements was of utmost importance, as the formation of a consolidated, joint, and united force was the only way to go for Operation Overlord, a complex operation which required the involvement of diverse units.

An instance in point was the British 6th Airborne Division that had been assigned to fix the eastern flank of the assault region. It, in turn, had to capture the Pegasus Bridge and the Merville Battery which managed to save the landings from enemy attacks. Special missions for these tasks were provided to the battalion while the leisure hours were filled with training during rehearsals and simulations that were designed to put them ready for the expected circumstances. The successful roll-out of these tasks scored the troops who underwent the training and were a major element of the strategic layout.

The American 82nd and 101st Airborne Divisions were given the task of occupying the key areas of the west in the beach, town of Sainte-Mère-Église, and the various road junctions. Their main goals are blocking enemy reinforcements from reaching the shorelines and creating secure positions that, if necessary, would shelter the advancing Allied units. The exercises for these divisions were so detailed and featured courses in city combat, the use of explosives to sink important facilities, and interrupt German movements. Their on D-Day actions on these beaches were clear evidences for their hard and good preparation and the strategic importance of their missions.

The involvement of parachutists in Operation Overlord was crucial for the general strategy of the landing. Their ability to hit the deep of the enemy occupied area, capture main locations, and cause disruption among the actors in the German army was an unavoidable part in the successful execution of the landing on the ground. The problems with these teams, their training, and their strategic objectives ensured that they were capable of the success of their missions being finely done. The D-Day airborne assault remains a symbol of courage, skill, and steadfastness of these elite soldiers, besides whose activities were the main element for the turning of the war to the side of the allies that at the end of that event got the victory.

Trailblazers of the Skies: The Pathfinders of D-Day

The successful deployment of the D-Day pathfinders was the main factor that secured the success of the airborne arm in Operation Overlord. Basically, they comprised advance troops and the procedure they had to execute was placing the markers of the drop zones that the main airborne forces would pass through, the paratroopers and gliders could land. They put their lives in the hands of some of the most advanced technology that the army had at the time, as they used for example radio beacons and signal lights which are basically navigational aids. Soldiers also used visual markers in addition to the which made it. The underground operation could not have come off if it had not been for the bravery and expertise of the pathfinders.

The contribution of the pathfinders was not only decisive but also very risky and endangerous. It was their job to jump into a hostile territory before the main force came there, this was quite often at night, and they would also have to mark the drop zones. This included connecting radio beacons, called Eureka sets, to the outgoing aircraft. Those bands of the radio waves. The pilots would be guided to target properly with these emanations. The pathfinders were using the visual markers alongside the radio beacons. The signal lights and panels were set up in locations that were specific to the drop zones. This technology was very important as it was the only medium that could work while the paratroopers and gliders would not land in the wrong places, thus the situations of uncontrolled dispersal and disorganisation would be avoided out of which disasters could arise.

The tasks and dangers encountered in this whole process were more than a little bit of the pathfinders' experience. They had to carry out the night sky assault in the area which was largely occupied by the Germans who were open enemies to the British and French participants. The key for them was reaching the objectives of the transportation plan which were the crossing over the land the Germans controlled and leaving the zones of tracking anti-aircraft by breaking the regulations and going through the windows of the sleeping military personnel. Furthermore, another line of the pathfinders when they got on the ground discovered being on their own and they had the task of setting up the markers as fast as they could and to keep away from enemy scouts. The risk of meeting German soldiers was very high every time they moved and any mistake could easily cost them their lives or their freedom if they were to be captured.

Extensive physical and mental ability, required to carry out the programmed, and combat proficiency was the pathfinders' percent exception. Their training underwent significant difficulties such as perfecting their parachuting skills in combat by giving practical knowledge about equipment handling, using maps for navigating, as well as adapting to the use of specific equipment. Moreover, their expertise was developed during training where they learned how to use a camouflage net to avoid being spotted and how to stay alive and finish their job in a situation that is not favorable or could be dangerous. A cool appearance and the ability to think straight under immense pressure were the distinctive features of pathfinder units, and their actions were significant only through them did the sky operations become operational without any failures or stalls.

Another of the pathfinders' harrowing missions evincing their daring is "Operation Overlord" on D-Day. Some of the many pathfinders from the 82nd and 101st Airborne Divisions of the USA and the 6th Airborne Division of the British Corps jumped in Normandy at the small hours of 1944, June 6. They were initially attracted to the idea of marking "drop zones" near exactly important locations using their Eureka beacons. For instance, sustaining the town of Sainte-Mère-Église, an area that served as a pawn to block German reinforcements from reaching the beaches is where the drop zones would have been. While some of the main events occurred under the cover of darkness and the atmosphere turned to be very tense due to enemy fire, the pathfinders were successful in setting their drop zones practically by using beacons and spotlights.

Not only did the pathfinders who were members of the 82nd Airborne manage to put the mark of Drop Zone A the pathfinders of the 82nd Airborne Division were also a successful team in setting up the markers for the Drop Zone near the town of Sainte-Mère-Église. They were hit behind their targets and in front of the German forces who sparked a gunfight with them, but they could gather around, place the beacons, and send signals to the incoming airplanes anyway. This allowed the main body of paratroopers to land and execute their action with precision on the town. The encirclement of Sainte-Mère-Église was a major win early in the fight for the Allies. They managed to disrupt the German communication and transportation routes. And also, the operation has served as a striking demonstration of the success of the pathfinders' mission.

In a similar way, the pathfinders of the British 6th Airborne Division were the ones who had the most significant part in the target marking of the drop zones assigned to those units which should take over Pegasus Bridge. This bridge across the Caen Canal was the key strategic target that should be kept well to gain security on the left side of the whole invasion area. The pathfinders faced hard resistance, beside the problems of the Normandy rugged terrain and managed to set up their markers that resulted in the successful landing of the principal airborne force. The subsequent capture of Pegasus Bridge by the British was a momentous achievement the closed off the eastern verge of the invasion beaches.

The pathfinders on D-Day were of course a part of some bottlenecks. Misdrops were one of those as soldiers had fallen off target points in the deep darkness of the night which helped to highlight the major issues involved in airborne operations. However, the pathfinders' capability to adapt and surpass were the only clear evidence of their improvisation and quick thinking. They often fought with German soldiers in order to secure their drop zones and show the correct way to the following waves of paratroopers and gliders.

The pathfinders' perspectives were more than just checking the drop zonnes. Their early arrival and the movement behind enemy lines caused some misunderstandings and along with that disrupted the German defensive plans. The psychological impact of the knowledge that the Allies were already executing their plans within their territories caused the confusion in the German Army, which was, nevertheless, one of the major reasons of the whole invasion's effectiveness. The pathfinders' will to fulfill their task under such incredibly hard conditions was the most powerful proof of their irreplaceable role in the overall implementation of the Operation Overlord strategy.

The pathfinders let us live eternally, who stepped beyond the ordinary stumbling paths entirely through their bravery, skill, and dedication. Their performance on D-Day was the epitome of the military operation intricacy where perfect coordination accompanied enormous risks. The pathfinders, to a great extent, brought the Normandy airborne assault into being, through their efforts modelled on the one of the RAF pilots who went first, broke the tunnel, then came back to drag the fellows. They must have been saved by the angels because you cannot imagine the difficulties they faced during that night. Another reason for the success of airborne forces in Normandy was that the pathfinders, which were crucial in the initial phase, made it possible so that the larger airborne and seaborne forces could be stationed and conducted efficiently after that. The pathfinders' saga is notable for valor, as it underscores the painstaking and perilous process that led up to the conclusion of one of the most decisive battles of the First World War.

From the Sky to the Battlefield: The Paratrooper Landings of D-Day

It was the case of the war between paratroopers that charged the Trojan horses with some of the greatest talent and motivation to operate in the province; operations like the one of the latter were hidden out of the enemy's view and were initiated in the volume of the French territory farthest from the coast, including the overhead aircraft dropping paratroopers. They have been meticulous in the preparation and also the implementation of these air drops, which have been included in the coordination of several factors in order to ensure the realisation of their goals. The pathfinders had started the process of the system by marking the landing areas and now it was left with the immediate paratroopers to execute their missions as reputable participants.

The parachute landings were a multifaceted operation that required the utmost concern. In this milieu, never had the American 82nd and 101st Airborne Divisions and the British 6th Airborne Division been deployed simultaneously. The priority was to transport three paratrooper divisions— the U.S. 82nd and 101st divisions and the UK VI Airborne Division—namely the three backside of the German troops in the early morning of the 6th of June, 1944. The foundation of the drop zones, along with their creation, played a big role in the accomplishment of the task. Planning and selecting tactical spots near crucial goals like bridges, road junctions, and the comms centers were the most important aspects. In addition, they also had to be easily accessible and defensible for the paratroopers that would enable them to regroup quickly and then attack.

The paratroopers were met with the pathfinders who were the only ones capable of help them out in the matter of managing a well-consolidated landing. The pathfinders, who were forward observers in the first wave, showed an amazing incredible ability as well as the state-of-art equipment - such as radio beacons and lights - to get to the right place and to show others the drop area. These transmitters generated light indicators to the airplanes giving them the correct location to land. These efforts, however, the paras were seriously hampered, because the factors such as the bad climatic conditions, anti-aircraft means, and navigation mistakes disseminated them all over a vast area, thus, they faced more difficult problems.

As a matter of fact, the chaos and confusion accompanying the paratrooper landings were very significant. A vast number of paratroopers that deployed found themselves distances from the areas where they were supposed to land due to which they were scattered all over the Normandy countryside. Parachuting in this way meant that small groups of soldiers were dispersed, yet the small, isolated groups were able to make their way through the land despite the treacherous conditions, by avoiding German patrols and seeking to join the squad. Survival in the dark was problematic as the soldiers could not recognise landmarks and disoriented themselves.

The prompt combats took place in the wake of the landings at night, and they were tough and had no order to them. It was a common occurrence for the paratroopers to encounter enemy forces right after the jump; thus, they were always in a gunfight to gain control of their objectives. The first attacks were decisive for the airborne invasion. The paratroopers' resilience and training were displayed when they managed to come back together fast, although they had landed in different places, and thus they performed a series of organised plays which were a true mark of their training and the level of resilience.

The 82nd Airborne Division made a significant breakthrough in the area of the paratroopers by capturing Sainte-Mère-Église. The town was really important because it was located on the main road leading to the beaches and the Germans used it for reinforcements and communications. Despite the fact that they were dropped out of their target and under continuous fire, the paratroopers found the town and they managed to secure it. Due to this triumph, not only were the enemy German movements curtailed but also the morale of the Allied units was uplifted.

The arrest of the bridges over the River Orne and the Caen Canal by the British 6th Airborne Division was also a considerable highlight. The bridges in question were not only the key but the only protection for the east coast of the landing zone of the invasion, and they also could prevent German fighters from reaching the beaches with their counterattacks. The enemy personnel were very deadly but will power plus adopting sophisticated tactics allowed the regiment to obtain and preserve these significant bridges until backups arrived. As a result of this action, the landing of troops on the beaches was shielded, and thus, the Allied forces advanced inland without interruption.

In addition to the 116th Infantry Division, the 101st American Air Division was another important unit holding key road junctions and breaking German communications. Their purpose was to secure the forks at Pouppeville and the nearby bridges, which were indispensably important for an allied transport of forces and arms. The jumpers came upon stiff resistance, fortunately, they were able to get through the difficulties by using a mix of surprise, speed, and aggressive tactics. They contributed to the victory of the invasion by stopping the reinforcements from coming to the German side of the beaches.

The paratroopers not only displayed great courage and adaptability but also showed their skill in improvising. The unit had to take the snap decisions in the course of affliction, sometimes one on one to other groups until they could regroup into larger units. The way they created and kept their morale up in such weak situations was the most crucial factor in their victory. Apart from achieving their short-term objectives, the paratroopers 'actions no less disrupted the German defensive schemes and even opened naval opportunities for their allies to take advantage of the situation as a whole.

The sagas of bravery and heroism among the paratroopers are quite a few. A lot of the soldiers exceeded expectations by example as they were the leaders of the fellow soldiers in assaults on fortified positions, retrieving the injured among the enemy firings, and securing very important spots with their limited resources. These acts of heroism and persistence were not only the central elements of the parachuting assault's success but also they are the greatest examples of military valor and thus the most remembered ones.

The paratrooper landings on D-Day were a critical moment in Operation Overlord. Their execution was the setting of the scenario besides chaotic circumstances, which was vital for the success of the Allied invasion. All of these troop men whether it was by rushing the target, cutting German defenses, or the evacuating crew was a story of their training, bravery, and resilience. They really made the day as they contributed greatly to the counterbalancing of the situation and the expulsion of German army from Western Europe.

Silent Wings: The Glider Operations of D-Day

Paratroopers on D-Day made use of gliders for aerial assaults; it was a strategic move incorporated which substantially boosted success in Operation Overlord. These unpowered planes, in turn, the heavier equipment, the vehicles, and extra troops were delivered to the battlefield, which was involved in landing. Paratroopers who had previously been deployed in the area were its greatest support. All of this crucially allowed the airborne units to take their missions with supplying the transportation of artillery, jeeps, and other materials that were necessary for the troops to have. The operation of the gliders served to, primarily, the goal of the paratroopers' successful landing by making sure that the airborne units possessed the weapons and mobility that would help them accomplish their missions.

The glider planes of Overlord were brilliant pieces of technology at the time when they were constructed. Made mostly of light materials such as wood and fabric, these vessels could glide silently through the sky after being taken by a powered aircraft, and then it would be released to parachute to the designated areas below. As for the American Waco CG-4A and the British Airspeed Horsa, these gliders are the most widely used models. The passenger planes had long-haul capabilities with a carrying capacity for troops, light trucks, ground attack guns, and supply logistics. The Waco

CG-4A could carry either 13 soldiers or a mix of equipment and workers in a small jeep; the Horsa could even carry a maximum of 25 soldiers or heavy equipment as such as jeeps and howitzers.

Due to the detailed loading procedure, balance and stability are the main elements that have to be considered while deciding the completion of the procedure. The load was always equalised to sustain the flight and the soldiers and other items were secure from any displacement that may occur during the landing process. The gang comprised of the infantry, sappers, medics, and other vital kit load and showed the diversified character of the airborne units regarding the type of support they gave. The gliders were connected to the sky by C-47 Dakotas in which they reached a proper altitude to be released in a setup that let them fly to the landing zones they were supposed to or crash!

Air mobility took its turn at the unpleasant load when glider operations were in the picture. The perilous process of getting these airplanes off the ground then to bring them back down again included a variety of hazards such as navigation problems, enemy fire, and the mere fact of landing on a sandy or unfamiliar airfield. The gliders were without engines, so they were especially susceptible to damage during the entire journey from the altitude to the landing phase. Pilots were required to use field-applied markers as navigation beacons, often relying on their visual senses only, and coming down in areas that might be impeded by hedgerows, trees, or other objects.

The particular example of Pegasus Bridge and Horsa Bridge was the fact that these two bridges were captured by the British 6th Airborne Division, which was a part of the whole operation of the glider forces D-Day. These two bridges over the Caen Canal and the River Orne were the most important ones for control over the eastern zone of the landing area. Gliders, loaded with troops and equipment, got into areas near the bridges early on the morning of 6th June 1944 and, although they were under very heavy anti-aircraft fire and the landing conditions were not suitable, they managed to do so. The successful capturing and defending of these bridges helped the West Alliance in the fact that the German troops could not approach the beaches and they were also protected from the east. The Fighter planes were able to execute their mission with the help of the gliders proving to be the most effective technique in supplying exactly what was needed for the ground troops.

Nevertheless, the glider operations were fraught with troubles. It was frequent that gliders crash-landed due to the complicated terrain and the few suitable landing areas. And there were instances in which gliders were shattered or damaged upon touchdown, thus, these resulted in casualties among the troops and loss of important outfit. To mention one, in the first attack on Pegasus Bridge, several gliders went beyond their landing zones or hit the obstacles, not on target causing some people to be injured and the attack to be delayed. The strong will and the well-honed pilot skills allowed them to reassemble and reach the goals in spite of the above-mentioned impediments.

Moreover, the operations of the glider also had to face the issue of navigation, which was very important. However, it was the glider pilots, who often performed in the low visibility or under enemy threat, who had to use their instruments and eyesight to find their landing areas. The these effectual of mission accomplishment depended on the ability of the pilots to adapt to the changes in the environment and make quick decisions. The glory and expertise of the glider pilots were of utmost importance in the troop and equipment reaching the designated locations.

The glider operations had a big impact on the whole success of the parachute assaults. By getting the access to the battlefield and pressuring the parachute units to fight, they did a great job. The approach of the gliders of silently and landing dropping off the men was both the innovation and the element of surprise. This, in turn, caught the German defenders off guard, thus, causing confusion and disarray among their ranks. The integration process was made flawless due to the glider operation, which was consistent with the broader strategy of the airborne troops in Operation Overlord, demonstrating the creativity and adaptability of the Allied forces.

To sum up, the glider operations of D-Day were a very significant factor in the airborne attack as it provided a lifeline to the paratroopers and thus powerfully assisted them in accomplishing their goals. The intuition from glider use, such as the web of creative designs that led to the transport of impressive tech, was both the curse and the boon of the operations which showed the intricacy and the importance of this side of the invasion. The glider operations also proved resourcefulness and valiance of the Allied forces, and this contributed to the success of the entire Normandy landings and the liberation of the Western Europe peninsula, and ultimately it led to the thanks we owe to them today for saving ours.

Shielding the Beaches: The Tactical Role of Securing the Flanks in D-Day Operations

Securing the flanks of the beachheads during the D-Day invasion was a mission of paramount tactical importance. Ensuring the protection of the seaborne invasion force from potential German counterattacks was crucial to maintaining the momentum of Operation Overlord. The airborne units, including the American 82nd and 101st Airborne Divisions and the British 6th Airborne Division, were strategically deployed to secure the eastern and western flanks, thereby preventing German reinforcements from reaching the beaches and creating a secure perimeter for the advancing ground forces.

We prove an apt term when we say that the significance of the flanks should not be minimised. The Allied generals discussed even before the invasion how the landing of the open beaches would bring only part of overall success while the other half of the strategy was the safety and protection of the new beachheads from sly and powerful German counterattacks. The sides were mainly in danger because they were the extreme ends of the areas on the shore. Here, the Germans could concentrate on their efforts, thus making it easier to pierce through the invaders' line of defense and drive them back into the water. Through the positioning of the airborne units in the most important places, the Allies intended to arrest any German move and so achieve the object of their buffer zone.

The zealous encounters at the start between the airborne troops and the German defenders wound up in tight situations and they found still numerous obstacles on their way. The paratroopers and glider troops mostly didn't land on the site as scheduled and so, they were dispersed throughout the area which was also under fire. The elite army forces met with an iron resistance of fully entrenched Germans. They were able to win over them only after using a successful combination of surprise, speed, and aggressive tactics. For example, one of the toughest challenges was when the British 6th Airborne Division, which was given the eastern flank to secure, had a heated engagement to capture both Pegasus and Horsa Bridges. These structures were strategic for the control of the eastern isthmus of the landings and their capture disrupted the movement of German troops and "blocked" them from reaching the beach.

The 82nd and 101st Airborne Divisions fought the same intense battle on the beach as the German air units. The primary mission of the American 101st Airborne Division was to hold the key road crossings and bridges under its control, and they were met with heavy German opposition as they swooped into the capture of the Ste-Mère-Église and several other vital points. As they struggled against the unexpected firing and coming together till they found the other units, the paratroopers, who came out of the sky at night, often had to move as if they were in small, separate groups. Their innate ability to maintain the initiative and keep pushing forward even in the lack of organisation was crucial to their victory.

The concept-to-battle synchronisation of the ground forces with the defense of the flanks was the fundamental tactic in the attainment of securing the flanks. Loved ones had to be provided with safe corridors along which they can land and eventually hook up with the beach-bound forces. This was possible through effective communication and joint military action between airborne and ground forces. The indicated communication methods of radio communication, runners, and pre-arranged signals held the key to maintaining the coordination. The knitting together of airborne and ground forces was a piece of cake that was successful, thereby, forming a united front to not only resist German counterattacks but also to widen the Allies' control in Normandy.

Containing the enemy and the offensive thrust of the German forces required to hold and increase the safe zones. At first, the objectives were to be reached and the airborne units then were to reinforce and plan for the German attacks which were considered inevitable. This consisted of constructing such things as trench systems, deploying defensive perimeters, and directing the necessary people to the points where the bridges, crossroads, and high grounds were. The jumping soldiers showed they implemented their skills and their will to stay in their positions as they pushed back the continuous German pressure by claiming the pieces in the battle again.

One perfect example to highlight the courage of our soldiers is the protection of the Merderet River crossings by the 82nd Airborne Division. With the help of the sky troopers, the barriers kept the Chinese out of their defensive positions and passed through to the beaches by the time troops moved inland. Holding their lines stopped the Germans from launching a major onslaught that would have constituted a potential risk to the entire western portion of the invasion process.

The role of the British 6th Airborne Division in guarding the eastern flank was also very crucial. On the one hand, they did so by taking the bridges of Pegasus and Horsa away from Germans who tried to grab them back many times. The paratroopers along with the fundamental glider and artillery support accomplished this feat by fighting off the more powerful enemy hoping to occupy the place as well as being bombed down by them. In the process, they established a strong defence whereby the eastern coast's segment between the two rivers was safe and thus the other two elements went on to join the British and Canadians on ground forces to push the German presence off the beaches.

Both defensive and offensive strategic measures were employed in the process of building up the already possessing areas. The airborne units scoured their perimeter, conducting patrols and reconnaissance missions to identify and neutralise any last German resistance that might be in the vicinity, besides launching localised attacks. The new units coming in fortified our flanks and the Allies even established the momentum to regroup and to get ready for further front and flank operations at surviving France.

The indomitable, adaptable, and relentless determination of the paratroopers in capturing the flanks was the most important thing in the general success of the D-Day landings. The creation of their safe healthcare environment was the environment in which seaborne forces, in the long run, could build up an insurmountable number in their beachhead with the result that they could advance along the coastal highway in Normandy and far beyond. The teamwork of the airborne and ground units, the intense clashes in the initial phase, the subsequent challenges representative of the criticality and variety of the issues were the key aspects of the his piece in the Operation Overlord campaign.

On the whole, the mission of the secure flanks was a hub in the success of the invasion of Normandy. The parachute troops' capability to do this, even though they had to cope with tough problems, was a manifestation of their importance and their effective training and planning. Their actions not only preserved the beachheads but also enabledt the lighting of the fire of the liberation of Western Europe, which marked the turning of the Second World War.

3

The Beach Landings: Sword, Juno, Gold, Omaha, and Utah

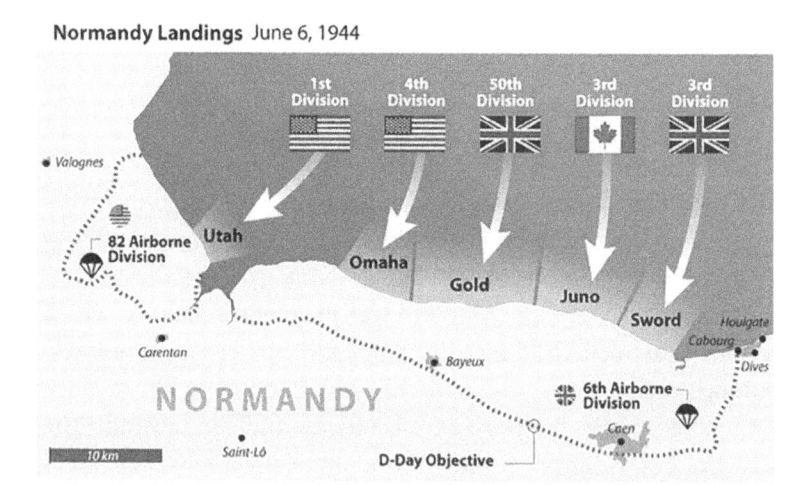

Normandy Landings June 6, 1944

The First Step to Caen: The Assault on Sword Beach

The sea-marked area of Sword Beach lay to the extreme east of D-Day's Allied incursion and therefore, the central location was vital to the successful liberation of Normandy and, eventually, Western Europe. The main goal at Sword Beach was to gain safe entry onto land and annex the town of Caen. This city, which was a strategically essential point to withstand capture by the Allied forces, as its takeover would facilitate their movement deeper into the country and eventually, it would have allowed them to proceed well beyond the borders of Normandy. The British 3rd Infantry Division, combined with elements of the British 27th Armoured Brigade, initiated the invasion of the local area of Sword Beach and was characterised by the high level of coordination and preparations.

The preparations for the penetration of the Sword Beach sector were highly specific and comprehensive. Major General Tom Rennie's British 3rd Infantry Division led the first assault. The regiment was supposed to land on the Queen section of Sword Beach and rush to take caen. The British 27th Armoured Brigade, armed with special tanks that were nicknamed "Hobart's Funnies," was assigned to the infantrymen to assist in beach obstacles and to provide fire support.

The planning incorporated troop and equipment disbursement in such a way as to ensure that a balanced and formidable assault force could be created. Troops consisting of infantry were to be the first to be landed with the engineers and armored units following them. The engineers were charged with the responsibility of clearing obstacles and mines to ensure the safe passage of both the tanks and additional infantry. There were also artillery units that were essential to provide supporting fire during the initial assault and after the subsequent inland advance.

The bombardment of the sea. The shore was necessary in order to overcome the German defenses. The bombardment had the purpose of wiping out or making inactive the bars, the guns, and the machine-gun nests of the Germans on the beach. This Stage showed that getting ready was a united effort of the naval and air forces of Britain which got the ships to attack directly from the sea and the planes to go to the places that were beyond the coast. Conversely, even though the bombardment was very strong, the Germans were still able to keep a big part of their defense, thereby the landing forces had a hard time getting through.

The first time the British landed on the Sword Beach was 7:25 in the morning on the 6th of June 1944. The adversaries of the troops came to them as the boats were just before the shore. The beach was strongly fortified, with objects like wooden stakes, mines, and barbed wire which were constructed to the landing troops. But, in spite of this, they had challenges that Britain's 3rd Infantry Division overcame while landing on the beach that were thrown out to sea by the Germans. The Sherman Crab flail tanks, and Churchill AVREs, tanks of the 27th Armored Brigade, that were specialised were the ones who did that by clearing away the obstacles and also providing the fire support to the infantry.

The combat witnessed by the German infantry was really intense. Machine-gun fire, artillery, and mortar rounds aimed at the landing troops were such a disaster that it led to a high number of deaths. Nevertheless, the bravery and steadfastness of the British soldiers did not let them down, and after all, they marched on the mainland through an area that is a salt marsh. The main tanks supported us at the time after the first landing which the difficult struggle to be established near the beachhead arose and move onwards to our main objective prevailed.

The struggle for Ouistreham was the most significant thing that took place at that time, as it had a population of a few hundred people living near the beachhead. Safeguarding the link to the east of the beach of the aforementioned town using Ouistreham was the most crucial part of it. The sight of the British soldiers trying to handle the bigger German forces instigating together in the protective positions was heart-breaking. The fight went on and was very violent with tanks playing the main role, not to mention artillery's use to warheads the lands and move the lines of defense. The gaining of the bridgehead and making the area safe for the continuation of operations was a big achievement to the success of the Allies.

Digging further into the territory the British 3rd Infantry Division got down to earth in the form of linking the ground units to the paratroopers of the 6th Airborne Division, apart from their position which was west of the area of aim. Through this, the British authorities kept the momentum up and made sure that the invasion strategy would happen as planned. The bridge locations and other crossing points were safe, as a result of the airborne units securing them in the area, such as the Pegasus Bridge, which controlled the ability of the eastern side of the beachhead to be entered. The particle binding was when the air and sea soldiers connected, the Allies managed to breakthrough and follow their set goals.

The development towards Caen, nonetheless, was time-consuming to get underway. Caen was the chief objective of the British due to such as it was the chief railway center, airfield, and a communication link. The German forces really had a strong hold of the city with the 21st Panzer Division being among the units that were stationed there. Moreover, the British troops went through resistance as they were attacked by the enemy from the guns on the walls, the tanks, and archery from the German forces and armored vehicles.

Considering the solid stronghold of the enemy, British forces managed to maintain their march. The progress was not continuous as there were several fierce encounters between Allied soldiers and Germans. The troops were trying to get closer to Caen, so they were forced to fight against the German army to destroy their defenses. The village should also be occupied to congregate stronger forces against the city and ready it for the final battle.

The main role of Caen for the whole Normandy plan was far from wordy. Its capture realised the winning of the war by the Allies and doing sabotage to the German defense line. The British 3rd Infantry Division and their allies, with the support of other units, took part in the combat operation at Sword Beach. The subsequent forward movement on land was a preparation for the upcoming liberation of Caen and the success of Operation Overlord.

The stirring of Sword Beach and the development in the inner part towards Caen served as an example to show the intricate level and coherence regarding such a fundamentally largescale amphibious operation. The soldiers' gallantry, British combined with the perfect statement by the command and the disciplined execution were the cause of the event?s success. The conflicts that occurred on Sword Beach were important to the army because they were the ones that helped create the necessary landing strip in Normandy, release Europe, and thus end the war.

Triumph at Juno Beach: The Canadian Contribution to D-Day

The Canadian 3rd Infantry Division was responsible for ensuring the security of this important battlefield and the first beachhead line during the D-Day airborne invasion. The main aspects of the operation in Juno Beach were the necessary consolidation of the beachhead and marching forward to Carpiquet and the Caen-Bayeux road- vital strategic points without which the Overlord operation would not have been successful. The detailed level of planning and negative coordination with the British and the United States have already been outlined by the Canadian forces, the meticulousness of the planning and the bit by bit nought, and coordination with the British and other Allied units were the keys that led to the As a result of their intensive training and effective use of various supporting blasts, Cdn. forces did well in their training of amphibious assaults of which one was the torch operation. This included exercises such as landings on a simulated beach, the naval and air support of the team, and the use of special instruments that could lob in things like the surmounted obstacles and fortifications.

The commander of the Juno Beach assault was Major General Rodney Keller who had commanded the Canadian 3rd Infantry Division. The division's area was divided into two main areas: Mike and Nan, and all the objectives that were to be met were in these two areas. It was a very long and serious phase because it was the time when there had to be many exercises which aimed at getting soldiers ready for the amphibian assault. These exercises, including some pretend beach landings, war with naval and air support, and the use of special equipment to assail with obstacles and fortifications, were the ones that took place during the planning phase.

The connective relationship between Canadian and British forces was crucial to the tactical planning of the operation. The Royal Navy played a crucial role by softening up the German defenses before the troops landed, by conducting a naval bombardment. The Royal Air Force made air bombings in the heart of Germany to the targets that were seen as major and causing a disruption of the fuel supplies. Moreover, the duties of certain units such as engineers and armored divisions were integrated with the landing force to ensure a balanced and an effective assault. The effectiveness of the AVR, amphibious tanks popularly known as DD tanks, was ensured by their provision of vital artillery support as the infantry dropped ashore.

The Canadians soldiers' woes, while invading Juno Beach, were too numerous and considerably challenging. Through a channel of meandering waves and mist that caused a number of delays the landing sparks were thrown into a chaos in their way. The weather was wild and the visibility poor so there were a number of units that landed on the wrong beaches. After having sailed on the beach, the Canadian men discovered bursting defenses of the Germans, which were made of hardwearing concrete bunkers, machine-gun nests, and artillery positions. The men had been on ships and mines had been laid with barbed wire and other such things to prevent the troops from landing.

However, the Canadian soldiers won through the obstacles as they substantiated their name for strength and determination. The frontline division soldiers, who carried the brunt of the fighting, were subjected to massive casualties from the enemy's automatic machine-guns and bomb detonations. Still, the fact that the

Canadian soldiers had attended proper schooling and preparation demonstrated its significance with their timely adoption in such a hectic situation. The dump team worked persistently all through the day to remove the barrier, and bore the route through the minefield for infantry and a unit of armored tanks. The technology advantage was specially adapted tanks. They used their side armaments to neutralise the bunkers and strongpoints.

The owning of the beach by the Canadian forces was one of the matters that they managed to perform with high speed; this was also the most critical gain. Even though the French had a resistance in holding the war by themselves, Canadians succeeded to take Juno Beach few hours after the initial landing despite the difficulties brought on by the weather, and also, it became a living example of the full-proof plan which set the benchmark of the absolute gallantry. This feat eventually enabled the Canadian forces to push inland and accomplish secondary targets, which included the taking of the town Bernières-Sur-Mer. The city was the first position to be secured, which is why it was a very substantial victory and gave a cutting edge when it came to further progress.

Canadians made their way to the Caen-Bayeux road and Carpiquet with an intense fight and numerous obstacles. The enemy, knowing that these territories had a strategic value, did their best to guard them, thereby delaying the advancing of the Canadian troops. Canadians, however, pushed on, with a will of steel, using a mix of infantry and tanks along with artillery bombardments to annihilate German fortifications. The achievement of these target spots is a very significant step for the Allies' overall strategy, as the cutting of German essential communications and supply arteries will means that the successful launch of any counter-attack will not be possible.

The success of these accomplishments at Juno Beach is huge. The rapid seizing of the beachhead and subsequent inland displacement were very important for the Allies' ongoing existence. Via the takeover of the required targets and interference with the

Germans, the Canadian troops at Juno Beach had a great hand in the global success of Operation Overlord. Their activities, not only in the immediate goals, but also, in effect, set the ground for the future liberation of Normandy and the defeat of Nazi Germany.

The experiences at Juno Beach were a proof of the courage, talent, and determination of the Canadian forces. Their potential to demolish these challenging issues and obtain key goals was the reflection of their good training and readiness. The interaction with British and other allies was the reason then that the assault was not only well-supported but also strategically sensible. The victory at Juno Beach was the most important piece of the puzzle regarding the whole invasion of Normandy, therefore, we can see clearly that each part of the plan was a key component in the overall strategy.

In conclusion, the Canadian handheld camera that projected the city to a different reality at Juno Beach was usually characterised by different varieties such as those accomplished."So, the commanding officer and his men in advance should look for it to establish the path which would enable the easiest movement and avoid jumping from the beach suddenly to the battle zone". The Canadian force in a record time developed the techniques to overcome those problems leveraging the resilience and strategic prowess, and thus finally securing a strategic landing sites and advancing toward the key inland objectives.

The victorious minute at Juno Beach has been a reality thanks to the Canadian 3rd Infantry Division that was completely involved in a wider Allied operation, which in turn made the opening for the liberation of Normandy as well as selling guns against Nazi Germany.

Taking part in the success of the D-Day, this operation showed the allies' shared spirit of cooperation and unity, and their determination to complete the mission was unbreakable.

Securing Gold Beach: The British Triumph on D-Day

Gold Beach, one of the five D-Day landing beaches, was an important element in the successful completion of the Overlord operation. The responsibility for securing Gold Beach went to the British 50th (Northumbrian) Infantry Division, which put at the top or their goals capturing the town of Arromanches and building a connection with Juno Beach and Omaha Beach. Not only was the right preparation and realisation of the landing at Gold Beach a new epoch in the military history of the British troops. By also combining it with the deploying of some units as the 79th Armoured Division which was with the "Hobart's Funnies" tanks, has even more revealed the strategic inventiveness and resoluteness of the British forces.

The Gold Beach operations were very systemic and covered all details. Major General Douglas Alexander Graham, spearheading the British 50th Infantry Division, was picked to direct the operation because of his division's wide war experience and the reputation it had already made. The army division had no doubts as to what their tasks would be, which would be to set the beachhead, capture the strategic city of Arromanches, and secure a link to the American forces at Omaha Beach as well as the Canadian forces at Juno Beach. Taking into account all these objectives was essential for the realisation of a cont... was essential for creating a continuous and defensible front along the Normandy coast.

Among the mission-critical were the units from the 79th Armoured Division led by Major General Percy Hobart. These special tanks were originally armed with some new developments, including tanks modified in various ways that were known as the "Hobart's Funnies" and these were designated to the beaches. The Sherman Crab flail tank, for instance, the AVRE Churchill tank, were two innovations with the former clearing the mines while the latter was equipped with the powerful petard mortars to demolish concrete bunkers. These specialised vehicles were crucial to the planning, providing infantry with the necessary support to deal with the different German fortifications.

The preparatory naval and aerial bombing given before the We can see that the AI language models on the web can learn common words and phrases just like people! When it comes to familiarising the unmanned unit with daily operations, it is the owner who teaches it to recognise and respond to its commands using blocks of code that are made with the help of artificial intelligence algorithms... landings on the Gold beach, had the objectives of crushing the Germans and minimising the hazard to the arrival troops. This is because the Royal Navy concentrated its battleships, cruisers, and destroyers to smash the barriers of the German land, sending round after round of the Germans', but also, the Royal Air Force targeting the inland defenses with their brutal bombs, making it very difficult for the enemy to get reinforcements as a result. However, the strong enemy defensive positions clashed with the effectiveness of the attack that was weathered by the given troops. The assaults were followed by a brief period when the British had gone back from the beachhead; still, the German casemates continued to keep up the offensive fire, so that in many cases the situation of the Chinese was becoming more and more perilous due to the resolute resistance of the Germans.

The landing boats were, still before the first light of 6th June 1944, heading to the coast of Gold Beach amidst terrible weather, like rough waves and strong current, acting as a true obstacle to the landing of the British soldiers. The first group of infantry was fought by German fighters, who were prepared and took cover under fortifications thus offering ground resistance. The massive fire of machine guns, artillery, and the planted mines made the area a kill zone and nearly impossible for the landing troops to pass. However, the resistance of the 79th Armoured Division's specifically designed tanks proved to be efficient in the weakening of German defenses, creating possible new routes, clear of minefields and barbed wire, and demolishing their bunkers.

The battle that took the heaviest toll was the seizure of the little village of Le Hamel at Gold Beach, one of the main actions on that day. The town's fortifications by the Germans, it was a large stumbling block in the path of the British units. The very first stage of the conducting was done by the 1st Battalion of the Hampshire Regiment, powered by tanks and artillery. With long-term strategies, the soldiers gradually took control despite heavy resistance. The battles took place in the streets during which many people were killed. Despite the strong enemy soldiers, the British managed to take and secure Le Hamel, thus preparing the other British troops for a series of further attacks inland.

Capturing Arromanche was a very critical primary goal for the British troops that were bearing down on Gold Beach. One of these harbours was the Mulberry Harbours of which Arromanches was strategically important as the site of one, the deployment of which was crucial to the logistical support of the Allied invasion. These ports were manmade and the basic function of them was to make the quick unloading of supplies, vehicles, and reinforcing troops very easy besides the fact that capturing well-fortified ports was no longer necessary. The right capture and defense of Arromanches allowed the building of Mulberry Harbour B, which served to be the mainstay in the Allied push through Normandy.

The position of Arromanches was important and actually consisted of its value as a target. The creation of the Mulberry harbour was one of the factors that gave a regular supply line, which was very important for the success of the Allied operations. This capability was Strategic and among its main benefits were that the Allies could increase their power and start subsequent offensives targeting deeper areas of occupied France, a chain of events that eventually led to the liberation of Paris and the downfall of Nazi Germany.

Once the British forces seized the beachheads, the principal thought became the interconnecting of beachheads which were next to one another to create a united and unbreachable front. A complete line of defense was created where the Canadians together with the

Americans assisted and supported each other that the ally could strike back to any German counterattacks. The task involved direct communication and the transfer of the soldiers and machinery that operated on the newly built beachheads. This coordination of the different roles was crucial for the general success of Operation Overlord.

The advance inland from Gold Beach was punctuated by further contacts with the German forces. The British troops, who were assisted by armoured vehicles and cannon, went to vital places such as Bayeux and Caen. These towns were central in the control of transport routes and the further advance to the interior part of Normandy. The battles that were fought during this part of the operation were marked by the intensity and the great spirits of both the attacking and defending forces.

The British soldiers on the Gold Beach were both tenacious and flexible here the key to their success in the face of adversity. Their securing the beachhead, capturing the main targets and linking up with other forces of the Allies showed how good they had planned their operations and how well they had executed them. Ways forward"s victory was not only the realisation of the D-Day immediate goals but also a preparatory basis for the subsequent operations to free the European mainland.

In short, the skirmish at Gold Beach was a very pivotal element in the D-Day invasion. The thought out preparation and the use of armoured units, that were made for Saturn to the development of a British link rather than the occupation of the Anglo-Saxons, and the final reinforcement of the armament caused the achievement of the first of the goals. This made possible the subsequent execution of the preparation of the Operation Overlord and the defeat of the German military aggressor.

Blood and Sand: The Battle for Omaha Beach

From the D-Day landings, one of the five assigned beaches to the Allies was Omaha Beach, which the American 1st and 29th Infantry Divisions held. The objectives of the two American divisions were to gain a foothold on the beach and to proceed towards the crucial Saint-Lô and Carentan. The landings at Omaha Beach were based on elaborate planning and training, nevertheless, the resistance given by German forces and the problems that the landing crafts faced made it a terrifying and blood-drenched conflict.

The Omaha beach operation was so detailed that it reflected the complex and huge operation. The American 1st and 29th Infantry Divisions, who were in control of the whole movement, were properly trained for their mission by Lieutenant General Omar Bradley. The planning used in this operation involved the setting of the ofprnaye and the intelligence gathering and naval and air support to soften German defenses. This particvular area was again divided into segments that should be attacked in order to expedite the assault, with every specific unit in the sector.

While the landing craft approached Omaha Beach at dawn on the 6th of June 1944, they encountered the unexpected rough sea and strong currents that resulted in delays and disarray. A lot of the landing crafts either got off path or flipped over, causing significant losses even before the troops had made it to the shore. The rough and rocky waters also added to the complexity when the amphibious tanks landed, some of them got sunk. The landing team lost some precious armored support.

At the dauntless seacost, the feisty American army had to face a fierce battle with authentic German soldiers who were almost impossible to dislodge. The German Infantry Division 352 was ordered to maintain the defense with a highly directed line of heavy bunkers, machine-gun nests, artillery emplacements, and minefields at Omaha Beach. The preparatory naval and air bombardment did not bring the expected result, and the big part of these defences were left intact. As the landing craft's ramps gave way, the warriors could see they were buffetted with a storm of explosive fire from the enemies whizzing guns and cannons. The outcome of this was severe losses.

Complex battlefield at Omaha Beach transformed the site into chaos and heavy combat. The American soldiers were motivated to take risks and leave no way to the enemy. The sea was prevented with certain pitfalls like the steel hedgehogs, wooden stakes, and barbed wire that in the aim of wrongly tiring the soldiers and guiding them into the killing. The pilot groups of troops experienced a terrible turnout as a result of which many of them were left unregulated and unprovided with leadership thus left with no solution.

The promoting difficulties, but the valor and zeal of the American forces accomplishing of thos was the transition. Few partially connected units of troops, who are most of the times in charge of junior officers and non-commissioned officers, embarked on their first attempts to solve some of the problems. Engineers boldly made ways that cut across the minefields and were isolated by the barbed wire under submachine gunfire. There were a lot of soldiers who have shown courage to knock out the machine-gun nests and pillboxes by risking their lives.

At Omaha Beach, Lieutenant John Spalding and Technical Sergeant Frank Peregory contributed to the success of their companies by following numerous heroic examples. Spalding made his way up the confined pathway and attacked the German position from the rear, while Peregory took a difficult mission, completely alone, and defeated the enemy, taking in more than 30 prisoners. These and others were the acts of courage of the soldiers that gave the chance to the German defenses to be broken.

The definite game changer occurred when the Americans were able to climb the bluffs along the beach. Firstly, they used Bangalore torpedoes to blow up the barbed wire and were then able to climb up the steeper cliffs. In consequence, the soldiers secured the high ground. From here, they were capable of fighting off the enemy soldiers much better and also they could start moving forward. The takeover of the bluffs was a determining factor as this allowed the Americans to send more soldiers and equipment ashore, thus, strengthening their position and allowing an uninterrupted offensive.

The utter significance of Omaha Beach in the whole invasion plan was outstanding. The Battle of Omaha was the major transportation link between the American forces landing at Utah Beach and the British and Canadian forces landing at Gold and Juno Beaches. The success in the link-up made it possible to have a smooth continuous battle line, thereby variations in the movements of the people and equipment.

Taking Omaha Beach was a risk because the beach was an open and well-sighted beach vulnerable to the Germans' artillery who had their heavy guns on the high ground. The success of Omaha Beach was the guarantee that the Allies were able to maintain the invasion's leverage by pressing the essential objectives like Saint-Lô and Carentan, which were the focal points of controlling communication routes and hampering German counterattacks.

Amid the horror and confusion, the battle for Omaha Beach turned out to be a driving force, a demonstration of the strength and resolve of the American armed forces. The initial arrivals were not easy; there were many emerging challenges they had to deal with, such as the unexpectedly powerful German defense and the troubles due to the rough seas. Nonetheless, 1st and 29th Infantry Divisions' soldiers, by means of willpower and fearlessness, could get through all those trials and make the beachhead secured.

The capture of Omaha Beach became a crucial momentum shift in the Normandy invasion. This opened the opportunity for the Allies to take solid ground in the continent launching their military operations to free Occupied Europe. The hard times the American

The Beach Landings: Sword, Juno, Gold, Omaha, and Utah

soldiers were through at Omaha Beach and their high casualty rate indicate the heavy toll it took on them. Nevertheless, their fearlessness and fortitude were paramount to the overall success of Operation Overlord and the ultimate defeat of the Nazis.

D-Day deepens and the Battle of Omaha Beach becomes the most respected and the most significant battle of the whole landing. The resistance that the American forces faced had actually become a measure of their persistence and determinedness. The triumphant completion of the tasks was a clear proof of the efficiency of the planning and the readiness of the soldiers at the front.

Omaha Beach has long been valued as a strategic asset extending its significance far beyond the area of the victory. This beach was the significant base for setting the supply lines and enabling the movement of the troops and the equipment into the inland. The beach was also used as a base for the troops to join forces with other Allies. The ability to form a tight and distributed front along the Normandy coast with the other Allies was an absolute requirement for a successful invasion.

Oboe Inlet has a record of gallantry and martyrdom. The bitter battle and major difficulties that the American units had to cope with the amphibiou's complication ans the threatened life-enjoyement of amphibears. The feat of Omaha Beach was completed through the perfect blend of the planning, the creativity of the strategies, and the will power of the foot soldiers who fought over there.

To put it simply, the Omaha battle was the turning point of the D-Day operation. The U.S. soldiers who stormed the beaches at Utah and Omaha also had to fight through many hardships and battles, but the bravery and decision of the troops resulted in a decisive victory. This accomplishment paved the way for the successful Allies' endeavor and thus the freedom of the Western Europe people from the Nazi atrocities. The story about Omaha Beach contains the acts of courage and self-sacrifice that the

American troops were made despite that of the defeat of Nazi Germany.

The Western Vanguard: Utah Beach and the Triumph of the 4th Infantry Division

Utah Beach, the westernmost entry point of the D-Day intrigue, operative for the freedom of Normandy was the turning point of the Allied tactics on D-day. The closing of the 4th Infantry Division, and the assigned areas of Utah Beach took in the beachhead and inland to connect for the aircraft units of 82nd and 101st Airborne Divisions. The invasion of Utah Beach was one which was prepared, guided by practically flawless technology, and was relatively calm if compared with ones on other beaches, which meant that a tone had been set for a prosperous inland advance.

4th Infantry Division, which was given the command of Major General Raymond O. Barton, was the body blockade that was chosen to carry forward the landing at Utah Beach, the reason being its strong army and a series of trainings. The landing at our beach was supposed to be a success only with the establishment of a perimeter, the exit routes providing the appropriate avenues of the operation, and the joining of the infantry and other units ahead of placing the united front. The primary way in which the plan was carried out was to advance quickly from the beach to secure critical points like Sainte-Mère-Église, an important locality for the overall control of the region road network.

With regard to the Utah Beach plan involving a detailed reconnaissance and a cutting of the naval and air forces, it must be said that the process was initiated from such a stage. The course to the beach was carefully designed, and amphibious tanks designed to be watertight (DD tanks) were used in addition to providing artillery fire and removing obstacles. By that means, their flotation screens tanks were able to sink onshore and participate in the battle against enemy weapons as well as supporting infantry with their arrival. Apart from that, the engineer units were assigned to demine the area and remove obstacles to enable the infantry to pass through without any delays or threats.

The operation faced unexpected resistance from German forces, the relatively light resistance from the enemy was the surprising finding. The massive bombardment staged by the Allied naval and air forces right before the assault was a real game-changer, eliminating the ability of the German defenders to a great extent. The 4th Infantry Division was greeted with less fire than was expected, which was a reason for a calmer and faster landing. The fact that it was so easy to land at Utah Beach was very different from the incredibly tough battles at the other beaches like Omaha.

The enemies of the 4th Infantry Division's became a whole lot easier as time passed as the men moved off to fight or got away. The helpfulness in use of amphibious tanks and quick work by the engineering units in clearing the areas through minefields and obstacles allowed the troops to get there. The soldiers were initially threatened by some Germans but they hotly neutralized these ones. The beachhead was without any particular sign of weakness and was captured quickly, and this enabled the division to devote more effort to inland objectives.

One of the notable accomplishments of the 4th Infantry Division was the successful connection made with the 82nd and 101st Airborne Divisions as commanded by the two airborne regiments. These airborne groups were airdropped in the back enemy territories with the purpose to secure main roads, bridges, and towns, thereby making German transport and traffic much harder and thus winning the beaches. Securing the link-up was an indispensable part of the all-invasion plan, ensuring the seaborne and airborne forces were on the same page.

The 4th Infantry Division was one of the first units to land on the beach and move towards the town of Sainte-Mère-Église, the key spot that had already been seized by the 82nd Airborne Division. By securing the town, the Allied forces would block the road networks and, in more simple terms, the Germans would be unable to get to the beach. The 4th Infantry Division and the airborne units held together a successful link-up in Sainte-Mère-Église. It was executed exactly, is, it was done with precision and thoroughness which allowed the advance inland to go swiftly and energetically.

The importance of this connection cannot be understated. With the seizing of the landings, the Allied forces gained an extra strength, which was used to construct a wall of defense that was never once shaken. This combination of teamwork of seaborne and airborne forces bore the brunt of German counterattacks. Besides, it was responsible for the prompt and continuous reinforcement of the units and supply of necessary materials. The effective link-up was a clear example of the flawless planning and coordination by the Allies which were the anchoring to the rest of the project's success.

The bounties accomplished at Utah Beach turned out to be indispensable for the overall victory in the Normandy combat. The 4th Infantry Division met more limited air and foot resistance and so was able to go on the beach and take over the no man's land with only a small delay. The proper use of amphibious tanks and specialized engineering units together with the ability to minimize obstacles development allowed yet another smooth course of all the events. The successful link-up with the airborne forces at Sainte-Mère-Église as the final safety measure further secured the Allied position and made the ongoing entering of Normandy possible.

It should be remembered that the operation at Utah Beach was a good example of detailed planning, coordination and adaptability in the war of the sea, the public. The involvement of the US 4th Infantry and the utilization of the airborne units had the final outcome of securing the western flank of the Allied invasion due to the success achieved. This was a considerable thrust for the fighting in Normandy, and it guaranteed achievement to the Allies which was indispensable for the subsequent liberation of France and the defeat of Nazi Germany.

Utah Beach is a story of strategic victory and operative officers showing their excellence. The Landings were relatively easy and advancing of troops inland was immediately started thus showing both, the efficient planning of the Allies and the toughness of the United States' soldiers. The successful realization of the objectives, landing operation at Utah Beach that was, was significant to the success of D-Day as well as to the broader campaign aiming at overcoming Europe of the Nazi occupation. The key to that unexpected victory that was critical to the struggle was the courage and persistence of the 4th Infantry and the airborne units.

4

Breaking Through: Allied Advances Inland

Beyond the Beaches: The Allies' Initial Breakout Efforts in Normandy

The time after the D-Day landings began to be the most vital stage of Operation Overlord, as the nonpareil time when the Allies had to change tactics from acquiring beachheads to town planning. The first assault was a time of many great difficulties for the Allies as they tried to form a more or less stable front, and with success pushed forward the great number of Germans who were quite tough in the defense. Opening up the beachheads was but the first step in the campaign to liberate France from the Nazis and to defeat Germany in the long run.

Right after the landings, the work of unifying the troops along the Normandy coast completed by the Allies had been so laborious. The main point was to make the coasts safe for landing which was the main job for the defensive forces and also the task of encirclement tactics themselves along with a constant trickle of manpower and equipment. The coastline had been divided into sprawls, and every individual had been situated in the division they represented. They were bonded together and it was on these sections that the first line of defense was defended and sustained.

For the Allies, the biggest issue dealt with was the necessity of running up against the perfectly-prepared German defenses lying on the other side of the beaches. The German soldiers had crumbled piles of rocks up, however, in front of they had planted znachitelnyeing of bunkers, minefields, and artillery batteries. These realities had to be methodically torn down to make way for the advancing Allied forces. The military situation after the first attacks proved to be very gloomy for the Allied army because the soldiers met with stiff resistance that was caused by the German positions dug into the ground.

To move from hitting the beaches to taking over inlands, different tactics were used. The use of all parts of the army including the infantry, armor, and artillery for example was the prominent one to get through the German fortifications. This kind of approach really gave the Allies a chance to put their superior fire power and mobility to work in the sense that they could break through the enemy[] defensive lines and []made the most of that weakness that the Germans had made defense. Moreover, the significance of aviation support was pointed out, when Allied planes were flying to hit the enemy's positions and supply lines and thereby such a measure was taken.

The effective occupation of key transportation routes and logistical centers was a major goal during the opening attack. In Normandy, roads and railways were the main traffic arteries for the thousands of soldiers, equipment, and supplies. The Alliance terminated those locations on the part of the enemy that were used for communication. They did it by capturing towns and junctions that were the most important in their communication network. In this way, not only was the movement of their armies made possible, but the enemy was also deprived of any chance to supply and reinforce their positions.

The primary goals of the initial breakout that were spelled out were actual. The occupation of towns like Caen, Carentan, and Saint-Lô was very critical for the logistics of the region as well as the contribution of the development of the Allied forces staying in the area. Beyond that, these were the central places that allowed the roads and railways to be connected and thus the Allies were able to extend control of the area. These struggles often lasted for a long time, there was a lot of urban fighting and numerous soldiers of both sides died as a result.

It is a well-recognized fact that the US forces had to secure the roads just as capturing the main towns became a priority. With the bocage or Norman hedgegrigs to slow them down, these are some of the many challenges that the Allied forces faced. These dense stands of bocage of two meters high and more that cross Normandy Blockers not only meant a favorable observance of the Germans but they also kept the Allied forces' mobility and visibility on a minimum. To achieve this end, such enhanced military vehicles as the M4 Sherman tanks, labeled "Rhinos" and having grass-piercing implements, were deployed to break through the native walls and open passages for infantrymen and other mobile armor.

Disrupting German supply lines was another key objective. The Allies pinpointed German logistics hubs, such as supply depots, rail yards, and road junctions, to diminish the enemy's capacity to sustain their defensive impromptus. This incident was settled with a ground attack, followed by an air strike intent to not only annihilate the main infrastructure but to create a situation of diminishing returns in the logistics. Along with cutting off the supply of German forces, the Allies also isolated their remaining lines with the result of weakening the Germans to fight back effectively.

It is not enough to emphasize the strategic importance of specific locations too much in the case of the Normandy campaign. From different perspectives such as military, natural, or geographical, the most important town Cane gives many different examples. That is what the German army had to experience. For instance, they had to supply their troops with already little rail & hide tamps as well as they had to fix their damaged road. The one major mile in the direction to Paris and other important areas in France was through its capture of Caen which was inevitable for the Allied forces to advance through France. Caen's struggle for control was one of the most challenging parts of the Normandy conflict involving different stages and a large number of both sides' assets.

Due to the strategic positions they occupied, Saint-Lô and Carentan weren't less important than the others. Saint-Lô was, in fact, a gateway to several major roads, and capturing it would permit the Allies to penetrate deeper into France. Carentan's strategic position, located near Utah Beach, was also of the utmost importance due to the fact that it connected the American beachheads and ensured the front was whole. The three towns, with their strategic significance, needed coordinated efforts and tough combats since the German troops were aware of their importance and had decided to defend them with all their might.

The successful breakout operations of the allies were largely dependent on the coordinated efforts of various units. The efficacy of the attacks synchronized by the attackers, the intelligence shared, and the backup provided by artillery and air cover were all important elements that permitted the overcoming of German defences. Efficient communication and command structures made it possible for the Allies to modify their tactics according to the changing battlefield conditions and to quickly answer German offensives.

Maintenance of the pace was an essential factor in the success of the breakout mission. Allies had to continue their move to avoid the Germans from reforming and reinforcing them with new defensive lines. This required the continuous supply of troops, equipment, and other materials to the front. The safe supply lines from the beachheads to the developing units were mainly logistics problems that required careful setup and execution. Besides the military equipment that was permanently mounted, the portable harbors such as the Mulberry harbors played a very big role in this development.

Apart from moving our own troops forward German counterattacks were yet another serious problem we had to deal with. The Germans declared a series of counteroffensives in order to expel the Allies off the beaches. The resistance of these counteroffensives was usually made by the best Panzer divisions and followed up by their support such as well - coordinated artillery with which Germany bombarded the enemy effectively and air strikes. It was the Allies who had to persist and change, moreover, they were on their superior side having more people, more posing power, and air authority adoption they finally fended off the combats. Key to retain the initiative was the capability to foresee and retaliate German attacks.

The plane breakout operations created the footspace for the further phases in the Normandy Blitz. The effective grouping of a steady and stable front line and the taking of the dominating positions enabled the Allies campaign to move extensively and get ready to carry out bigger operations such as Operation Cobra. The triumphs in the beginning also led to a great psychological effect by awakening the spirit of the Allies soldiers and confirming real prospects of a long-term offensive against the Nazi as well.

The strategic and on-the-ground requirements met in those of the earliest days could be the turning point of the Normandy intervention. The aim of the establishing of the coastal regions, moving further into the mainland and cutting off the Germans from getting food from there provided the basis for France to be freed of the Nazi rule and Germany to be defeated. The initial breakout efforts testified to the grit, creativity, and willpower of the Allied army which was able to withstand the overwhelming obstacles to reach the set targets.

Finally, the litany of events post the landing of D-Day in Normandy signified an important stage of the Normandy campaign. The attaining of the beachhead, the capturing of key towns, and the disruption of German supply lines were all the necessary conditions for creating a stabilized front as well as for the continued movement. The combination of different Allied forces, the capacity to keep up their strength, and the endurance in the German opponents' attack were considered the main points of these accomplishments. The victorious acts of the Allies in this process were indeed the groundwork for the bigger strategy in the liberation of Europe from the Nazi's power.

The Battle of the Bocage: Navigating Normandy's Natural Fortress

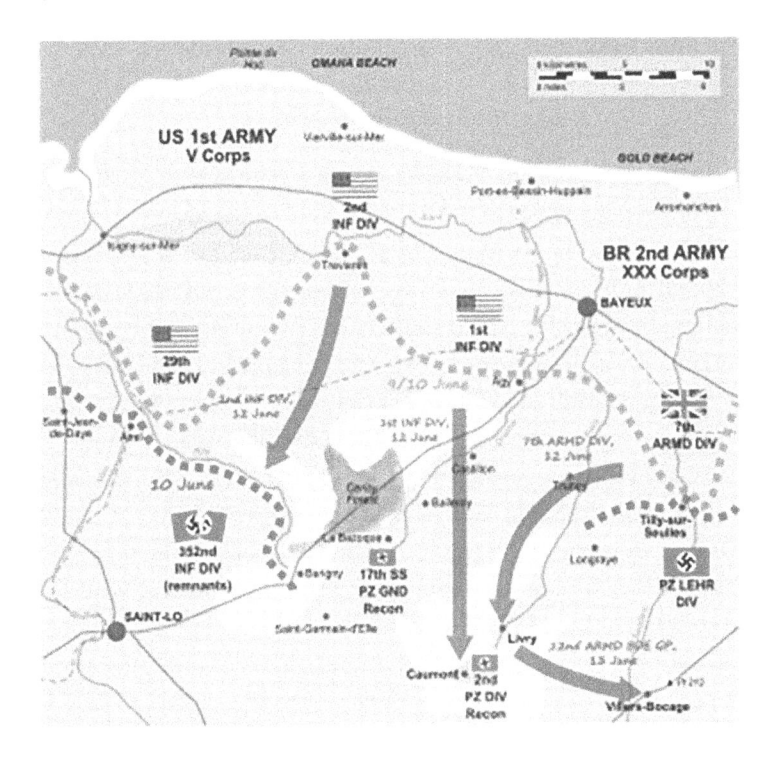

The Battle of the Bocage proved to be one of the most challenging tasks the Allied forces had to face after the D-Day landings. The hedges of Normandy, a.k.a. bocage, was a special kind of natural and very wild place that to a great extent hampered the war of the Allies. These thick hedgerows and small confused lanes were the Germans' main defensive positions along with the Allies' need for a new approach to the situation.

Concerning the bocage, the terrain was a block of fields followed by high thick hedgerows that were noted as one of the characteristics. These hedges were like around two and a half meters and a quarter of a mile around. That is, using the ancient and now over-grown hedgerows was a good tactic for the German defenders to block the advance of especially the tanks and infantry. The narrow paths however made maneuvering quite a task and in a way fostered paths that were really suitable for the Germans to ambush. The limited perspective and narrow paths resulted in the Allies being easily faced with the strong German attack.

The bocage was for the German protectors a natural fort which was easy to defend. Since the barriers were so dense, it was almost unreal to detect the Russian soldiers. They used greenery to create such well-hidden and well-protected positions that they became problematic spots for Allied soldiers who could easily become the prey of enemies lurking in the woods. The opposite side, however, was well-prepared due to the fact that the thickets, perhaps, and sniper positions were established with the ultimate possibility of the enemy being unseen. The Germans, identified by the victory won over the channel, also restricted the Allies' access and began to build what became the "Atlantic Wall" from Denmark to Spain. There is a high probability that fulfilled relatively quickly or moderately well in different nations while adopting different strategies was also contributed about relationship improvement in defense.

Battle in the bocage meant the matter of life and death for wars that came in and fought in very close quarters and always kept their eyes peeled. With the dense covers and the narrow tracks making the task of Allied units hard with communication remaining one of the major points of their struggle. The soldiers had to literally crawl at a snail's pace and be extra cautious and mostly rely on hand signals and messengers to control their movements. The potential for the ambush was always there, so they had to stay alert and be ready to get into immediate and fierce firefights.

To do this the Allied forces had to quickly find new tactics and make changes to combat and use them. One of the foremost things was when the Sherman Tank Rhino was firstly used. These tanks were equipped with a machine that would breach hedges which was in fact a kind of a horn made of steel cutting through the thick hedges. This process enabled tanks to open up passages for the infantry and other vehicles, in the process destroying German defences.

Battle of the Bocage provided a new perspective and a serious one, on the result of collaboration among the operations of combined arms. The infantry, armour units, and artillery had to join one another in the sharpest cooperation in order to battle through the German defenses. Infantry was to resolute close gaps immediately after eroding through existing row of hedges switched by tanks and artillery who gave them the direct support. The efforts of the elements of artillery and the infantry who used to fire lateral support guns lays ahead of them allowed them to minimize-known or possible-German positions to the extent of the suppressing enemy firing and hence protecting the moving of infantry.

The Allied forces faced a steep learning curve, but they were able to quickly and efficiently change tactics. In the beginning of the campaign, the Allied units lost a lot of troops because they were finding it hard to bow to the street crossing. Nonetheless, with the knowledge and the creativity they have, they can create more strategic plans for themselves. For example, small unit tactics grew increasingly important, while platoons and squads operated individually but worked tooth and nail to win out the German posts. Flexibility and rapid adaptation played the most crucial role in winning the bocage warfare which was previously very static.

The method of "fire and movement" was one of the best examples of these newly formed tactics. Unknown to the enemy, the infantry also used fireplace to close the spaces that separate them. First, a group of soldiers behind the scoring got ahead under the cover of suppressive fire from their allies, leapfrogging f with the enemy and killing the enemy. In fact, the tactics required tight coordination and communication but proofed to be effective in the bocage constricted the area. Also, engineers were a major part of the combat, ruining paths with explosions and bulldozers which were too thick to be just taken out.

The importance of leadership and individual initiative in the lower echelons of command increased in the bocage. Lower-level officers and NCOs had to make quick decisions at the front and were often unpleasantly taken out of their ease in distance firing. The aptitude to guiding the small unit well and immediately reacting to the threats was the cornerstone of the task to be accomplished in the environment with high friction.

It was at the Battle of the Bocage that intelligence and reconnaissance played a pivotal role, in the very beginning. It was a necessity to detect the positions of German fortress and develop the terrain because these were the main considerations for the planning and effective execution of the attack. A group of scouts and reconnaissance units were given the job of collecting all the necessary information about the enemy positions and the structure of the hedgerows. It facilitates the commanders then to map out a plan and organize the attack with greater precision.

The novel thinking behind the Armoured Assault Vehicle and the Allied campaign in the woods of Normandy were the high points noted in the aspect of innovation and adaptation. The data collected during these campaigns were used in the next effort on the breakthrough and the move to Saint-Lô and Caen. The bocage, which is a natural fortress, was impossible to breach but the fact that the Allies succeeded was due to the inevitable will of the victorious.

In essence, the Bocage was the stage that passionately underlined the Normandy campaign, a place that was known for the density of hedgerows and the narrow lanes between them. Among the methods employed by the Allied forces in beating these insane odds, the adaptation and innovation of Allied tactics by including the use of specialized equipment and conducting allied arms operations, were the most crucial. The incidents and the information learned from the bocage were consequential in the furthering of the Allied ship, finally contributing to the French liberation and demise of the Nazis.

Operation Cobra: The Breakout from Normandy

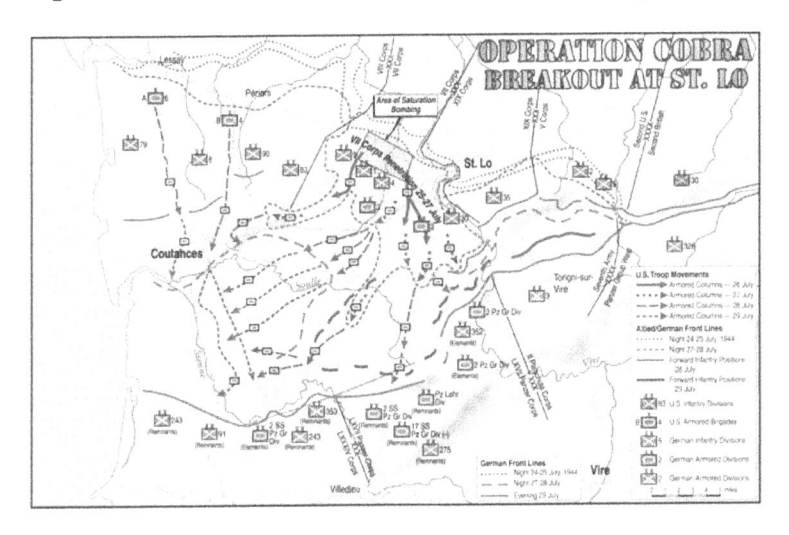

Operation Cobra was a very important attack that the Allied forces used to break out of the front line at the beachhead of Normandy and go in to the rural part of France quickly. This break-out masterpiece, imagined by General Omar Bradley and accomplished by the American 1st Army, had the intention to achieve a demolition of the German loopholes that had in fact been an obstacle to the moving the D-day since the very start. The tactics and the operations of Operation Cobra were extremely precise, which included thorough and ground-breaking preparation, highly effective use of aerial bombardment, and a warrior who was determined to utilize every single advantage that the battlefield could offer.

The United States commissioned Operation Cobra of the military battle plan as an essential turning point the day after D-Day was the catalyst of its attack Cerberus. The site of the Americans transformed into a perfect target for this secret operation, focused on laser weapons and guided by a network of software directions and machines. This operation was an attempt to break the line of Germans who had surrounded themselves, therefore, creating a way through which the American forces could quickly get to the interior of France and then to Paris. To do this, they had to defeat German troops who were very well situated and fancy, as they had successfully protected themselves during previous Alliance attacks.

A striking feature of the tactics was the organization of massive aerial attacks which would give the troops safety and grounds before the Germans could recover from the explosions when the infantry started to move in. The main term was an aerial attack that thousands of anti-German Allied aviators made at specific sites up the perimeter near a town named Saint-Lô. The air strikes focused on destroying German fortifications, killing or wounding the enemy soldiers, and causing a violent attack that would facilitate the army's walk-through. The use of airpower in such a strong and united manner was a novel idea but was risky as it required precision in avoiding friendly fire and at the same time delivering the most impact on the opponent's position.

On 25th July 1944, the drop bombing missions set off the start of Operation Cobra, which was a significant event. The skies over Normandy resounded with the sound of engines as numerous bombers emptied their payloads on the German lines. An incredible amount of destruction took place, where complete sections of the front line were erased and German units were embarrassed and thrown into a panic. Following this preparatory bombardment, the surface operation was carried out, and this was soon after the bombing was over.

The first attacks as part of Operation Cobra were run by the US First Army, which was comprised of armored and infantry divisions. The 2nd Armored Division and 1st Infantry Division were the vital areas in the first stage, and they occupied the spaces that the bomb sites created to breach deep into the enemy line. The success of kind of air and artillery preparation was clear to the American forces that met with far fewer obstacles than was expected thus enabling them to move speedily.

Furthermore, the Allies, by their further advance, aimed to take advantage of each breakthrough, passing away through the German lines and pushing the front further out. The German forces, although damaged by the bombardment, still were not in a good position to defend themselves. The use of the combination of arms that is including tanks, infantry, and artillery was a successful strategy for keeping up the momentum of the attack. The territory, at first, boasting the thick hedges of bocage, was a minor hindrance for the Allies as they shifted into the more open countryside.

One of the principal fights that happened during Operation Cobra was the fight for Coutances town. Coutances was a crucial connectivity center, and liberation of this site was decisive for Alliance movement. The 4th American Armored Division, operating along some infantry units, coordinated the simultaneous attack on Coutances, besides that were the Germans who resisted them and secured the town. The significance of this achievement laid in the fact that it shattered the German supply lines and command structures which in turn weakened the resistance of the Allied Forces.

The great success of Operation Cobra was, however, highlighted by the encirclement and eventual destruction of large German forces. The Falaise Pocket, was a result of the tactful convergence of the forces of Americans, Brits, and Canadians, of more than tens of German soldiers. The following clash led the Allied forces to the victory, which was not only decisive but was also dearly paid, with many German soldiers being killed in the battle and the others being held captured. This encirclement definitely was a breaking point for the Germans in Normandy, which resulted in the liberation of Paris and the following liberation of the rest of the country by the Allies.

General Omar Bradley's authority was a key characteristic in the successful progress of Operation Cobra. His wise judgment and skill of combining several complex operations that involved a number of units and forces were very much important in achieving the breakthrough. The contributions of the American 1st Army, as well as the British and Canadian forces, were the best proof of the effectiveness of the cooperative efforts and the perfect integration of various armed forces' capabilities.

Operation Cobra was indeed a very significant event during the Normandy campaign. This operation was the turning point in the war, which used to be the war of attrition, to the quick and definite advance. The decline of Germans' defense in Normandy forced the way for the Allied forces to move quickly to Paris, thus, liberating the towns, and cities in the journey. The achievement of Operation Cobra urbanized a psychological impact of equal weight with the waking of slumbering Allied morale and a litmus test of the continuing effectiveness of their strategy and tactics.

Rigorous planning, collaboration, and great performance were on the table for Operation Cobra. By using extreme bombardment from the air, effective ground attacks, and the never-ending use of breakthroughs, the Allies were brought to a victory. The operation's achievement were not only the necessary assistance to the rapid move into the French interior but also the preparation for the Europe later being liberated from Nazi occupation. The lessons and the tactics shown in the Operation Cobra contributed to the successful operations and would continue to do so throughout the lasted part of the Second World War.

Allied Coordination and Challenges in Normandy

The victory of the Allies in Normandy would not happen if the strong tactics on the battlefield only, but together with the operations of the involved logistics fields that supported everywhere would be fail in the broader provisions of help<a> style='color: #f00;'>. As the Allies continued their advances from the Normandy beachheads, keeping the advantage and safe supply lines were the major troubles. Continuation of the flow of reinforcements, equipment, and supplies was the fundamental condition to supply the expanding front and to secure the continued movement of particular key strategic targets.

The Allies' "master of supply" task was to fight ever more critical challenges to the needs of the business enterprise and to show was the most significant battle of Normandy. The ensconced beachheads, initial to all, no doubt, advantageous factors afterwards needed speedy coli for the troops pushed further in a rapid and secure manner. This was a blockade of the ports, airbases, and transportation routes that are used to bring the fresh reinforcements and materiel into. The Mulberry harbours, those temporary portable harbours that were built at the Gold Beach and Omaha Beaches, were very instrumental in the discharging of cargo ships and provision of a number of resources.

One of the major objectives of the Allies was the capture of the key ports, including Cherbourg. The importance of Cherbourg's deep-water port could be seen from the fact that large amounts of supplies and reinforcements were processed through it. The battle for Cherbourg ensued and the American units were met with the enemies in forts. As a result, gaining of the port certainly brought about a remarkable increase in the throughput of the supplies that, in turn, truly helped them to maintain the attack. Moreover, having taken over or created the airfields in the liberated zones also technology was the key to giving air support to the Allies and to arranging the materials to be supplied to the various operational units.

For moving a large amount of equipment and forces, the subject of inter-Allied communication and inter-Service cooperation was of paramount importance that namely was successful in solving these tasks smoothly. The American, British, Canadian and other Allied troops' integration and communication led by the command, which required a great degree of communication and cooperation. Coordinated and regular command and control structures and meetings were prioritized to the extent that they were the essential tools for proper allocation of resources and products of strategy-setting devices. General Dwight D. Eisenhower through the Supreme Headquarters Allied Expeditionary Force (SHAEF) became the main commander over all the operations, which in turn strengthened the unified structure that made successful actual and relatively fast decision-making possible.

Obstacles were also met by the Allies as the Germans counterattacked. Advanced by the Allied forces, German governors launched a number of counteroffensives to step down the pace and push the forces turned back as the part of a too rapid offensive. A major contribution from that era was the Battle of Mortain which took place in early August 1944, which was called Battle of Mortain. A German offensive was designed to cut off the American forces and re-attain the initiative by the town of Avranches, a vital point of the Allied supply lines was after recaptured.

The fight at Mortain was characterized by tough fighting, with the Panzer divisions of Germans as the protagonists of the clash. Despite initial gains, the German forces were met with a big army in the face, the defending American 30th Infantry Division and other supporting units were unbreakable. The usage of superior speed and firepower by the Allies was the key factor for driving out the German attack. The forces of the United States took advantage of their powerful armoured vehicles and artillery to interrupt the movements and destroy the Panzer units which were attacking them.

One more support that was really important in responding to the German counteroffensive was aerial help. The air superiority of the Allies made it possible to carry out continuous aerial reconnaissance, close air support and to hinder the German supply lines. During the Battle of Mortain, Allied fighter-bombers were in charge of the Germans' tanks and supply convoys thus, their force to be the offensive was seriously diminished. The synchronization of land forces and aircraft units was the key factor in attacking the German counterattacks.

The actions such as the readiness and flexibility of the allied forces were the underlying qualities shown in all of these people. Although they had to face the fierce resistance of the Germans and at times the life-and-death struggle, the Allies were able to re-group themselves on a regular basis, restructure their methods, and exploit their nominal mobility and firepower to an optimum level. The ability to give timely responses to the changing battlefield conditions and to decipher intelligence from a variety of sources were the essentials for the Allies to maintain the initiative.

The movement of supplies and the internal control to keep the Normandy campaign going was a behemoth task. The Allies were responsible for coordinating the flow of supplies through the English Channel, protecting the communications, and ensuring the front-line troops received the support they needed. The setting up of forward supply depots and the use of ingenious logistical solutions, such as the Red Ball Express, a truck convoy system transporting supplies from the Normandy beaches to the front lines, were the key factors in boosting the advancing forces.

[Output text]:One more support that was really important in responding to the German counteroffensive was aerial help. The air superiority of the Allies made it possible to carry out continuous aerial reconnaissance, close air support and to hinder the German supply lines. During the Battle of Mortain, Allied fighter-bombers were in charge of the Germans' tanks and supply convoys thus, their force to be the offensive was seriously diminished. The synchronization of land forces and aircraft units was the key factor in attacking the German counterattacks.

The actions such as the readiness and flexibility of the allied forces were the underlying qualities shown in all of these people. Although they had to face the fierce resistance of the Germans and at times the life-and-death struggle, the Allies were able to re-group themselves on a regular basis, restructure their methods, and exploit their nominal mobility and firepower to an optimum level. The ability to give timely responses to the changing battlefield conditions and to decipher intelligence from a variety of sources were the essentials for the Allies to maintain the initiative.

The movement of supplies and the internal control to keep the Normandy campaign going was a behemoth task. The Allies were responsible for coordinating the flow of supplies through the English Channel, protecting the communications, and ensuring the front-line troops received the support they needed. The setting up of forward supply depots and the use of ingenious logistical solutions, such as the Red Ball Express, a

The significance of keeping the operation in progress and making sure that supplies are available cannot be overstated. The conduct of operations to withstand the German enemy and their restoration is the key to success for the whole campaign. The good organization of different Allied units and a complete understanding of the possible logistical problems made it possible for the Allies to keep moving forward and, consequently, to free Paris and breakdown the Western European German fortifications.

To sum it up, Allied coordination and logistics during the Normandy campaign were the main driving factors behind the invasion and subsequent operations' success. Sustaining the speed, getting the traffic in place, and stopping the Germans from their counterattacks demanded an extremely high level of teamwork, creative thinking, and resilience. The possibility of integrating different units and conducting more complicated tasks was the proof of strength and efficacy of the Allied coalition. Through these actions, they not only enabled the immediate triumphs in Normandy but also set the stage for the later European liberation and Germanic defeat.

Turning the Tide: The Liberation of Key Towns in Normandy

The liberation of key towns during the Allied advance from the Normandy beachheads into the interior denoted the most important of many the campaign engendered France back to life and won the final battle with the Nazis. The main triumphs at Saint-Lô, Caen, and Cherbourg not only established their positions as the strategic linchpins but rendered an enormous positive feedback and impetus to the Allied forces. The towns, which were very important in their individual ways, were instrumental in the successful carrying out of Operation Overlord, hence the subsequent Allies' advancement towards Paris.

Saint-Lô, also known as the "Capital of the Ruins," was conquered by the Allies and became a primary target of the Germans. Saint-Lô is strategically located at the intersection of a number of major road networks, so its liberation by the Allies was an absolute necessity for the safe and timely movement of troops and supplies. The battle of Saint-Lô featured very heavy fighting especially with the Germans causing enormous structural damages. The American forces, in the foreground the 29th Infantry Division, confronted the heavily armed German opponents that were, reportedly, spread over large areas. Eventually, on July 1944, the Allies conquered Saint-Lô and thus, paved the way for them to take the critical logistic routes needed and then to attack the French mainland after they completed the breakthrough out of the Bocage Normand.

Caen, the other strategic city, that was secured, was initially the number one target of the western front operations. Opening onto the Normandy interior from its east side, Caen commanded the main points of entry into the devoted transport and logistics city, therefore, was the centerpiece of the plans. The battle of Caen among the most protracted and fierce ones marked the Normandy campaign. Under the command of General Bernard Montgomery, the British and Canadian forces got involved in this battle faced a strong German defense of the 12th SS Panzer Division, which was anchored in the western part of the town. The successful take-off of Caen made it possible for I. The use for both the sending of the F., further they also controlled the environment of the place. The city was conquered in August 1944, only after the many long and bloody battles. The Allied troops' capture of Caen allowed the Allies to form a solid stronghold and therefore, they moved towards the Seine River.

Cherbourg, which is a very important port city in Normandy, was another key goal for the Allies. The taking of Cherbourg was a requirement for the Allies to acquire a deep-water port to be used in supplying the logistic needs of the Allied forces. The fight for Cherbourg was characterized by very heavy infantry combat, which saw the Americans, especially the 4th Infantry Division, attacking the well-fortified Germans and the fighters who showed strong determination. The capture of this port in the late June of 1944 was a very essential strategic point in time for the Allies as it enhanced their ability to bring in the crazy amount of supplies and reinforcements that are enough to accomplish the whole action. The repair of the port facilities at Cherbourg was a turning point in the supply of allied forces with war materials necessary for the push towards France. This enabled the allies to continue into the occupied parts of France even further.

These freed towns' impact had been so great that the Normandy campaign as a whole and the wider war effort were entirely transformed. Not only did each victory send strategic advantages but it also raised the spirits of both the Allied troops and the French prisoners. The splendid capture of the very important towns of Saint-Lô, Caen, and Cherbourg has shown the inevitability of the bringer of the strategy and the makes of the army whose responsibility is to show the strength of the soldiers, therefore they are the ones that build confidence and pace of the campaign through other steps.

As the Allies conquered more territories, the weakening of the German defences was becoming more and more obvious. The loss of the strategic towns and transportation centers as well as the activities in the German supply lines and the proper execution of orders were causing problems to them, that is why they did not manage to perform successful counterattacks. The outcome of these successful battles was the constant erosion of German defensive power in Normandy, thus leading to the development of more complex strategies such as Operation Cobra, which was a breakthrough operation targeting to aim at the weakened German positions thereby, moving to Paris.

The quick and contiguous advancement of the Allied forces was a point to note of the liberation in question. The French traffics had secure the Allies into the five Le Mans incited them to reach more comprehensible. The fall of Saint-Lô and the subsequent breakout allowed for rapid advances through the open countryside, while the capture of Caen provided a strategic anchor for operations in the eastern sector of the front. Cherbourg was the only port to have an open continuous flow of supplies that ensured that the moving troops were fully supported and equipped.

These victories had an important psychological aspect for the forces of both sides such as the Allies and the Axis. To the Allies, the successful ones indicate that their strategy is right and the fear of being conquered has not left. The German defenders have lost morale by giving up important locations and their occupation of France is on the verge of termination. The steady advance of Allied forces and the liberation of French towns and cities ignited hope and resistance among the local population, further undermining German control.

The tactical and strategic values of these towns were not only limited to the particularity of the immediate battles. Each win was an essential part of a larger aim of capturing Paris and later attacking the land that was dominated by the Germans. The capture of Saint-Lô, Caen, and Cherbourg paved the way for the subsequent Allied advance towards Paris, ending in the liberation of the city in August 1944. This momentum continued to build, ultimately leading to the collapse of German defences in Western Europe and the retreat of German forces towards their homeland.

In short, it is the liberation of important towns like Saint-Lô, Caen, and Cherbourg that really was the only way the Allies could arrive into Normandy. These successes opened up strategic alternatives, disturbed the German defenses, and boosted the spirits of the Allied soldiers. The speed and luck of these progresses made them the immediate steps towards the final goal of the liberating of Paris and of France. The activities and sacrifices of the Allies in these combats were the decisive factors that turned the tide of the war and ensured the victory in Europe.

5

The Push to Victory: Liberation of France

Encircling Triumph: The Battle of the Falaise Pocket

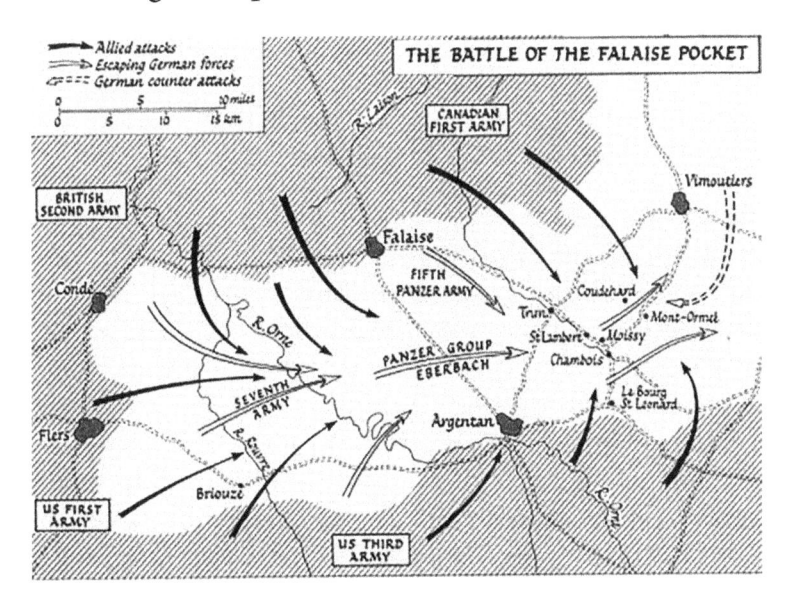

The Falaise Pocket battle was a turning point in the Normandy campaign during the fall of 1944. It seems that that was the moment when the Germans were willing to give up their position to the Allied in Normandy, which eventually led to the French liberation. This strategic opportunity being the key to a very critical type of warfare, which was mainly involved with American, British, and Canadian forces, was really a genius of strategies, with people believing that there was the only left way of possible formation, that was to catch and kill the Germans running away, and it was led there. The fierce combat, various cooperation, and the force of will among the Allies developed a large win that definitely changed the course of the war.

Strategic planning of Falaise Pocket took shape in the middle of a peaceful blast out of the breakout from the Normandy landing, which was still fresh in their minds, especially when the storming of Operation Cobra was over. The Allied leaders werecaught napping when they observed an opening which was ripe for be seized to get the retreating Germans. The idea of two-fronts approach, with the northern sector to be operated by the Britons and Canucks while the Yankees deal with the southern sector, was worked upon. The intent was to have troops from both sides advance from the opposite sides until they meet in Falaise thereby isolating the besieged Germans that had been surrounded by them.

The idea behind the drive to surround the broadband the perfect execution of the same[] was the proper coordination of movements and the launching of attacks at the most optimal moments. It was inevitable that the main attacking parties-Caunadian 1st Army, under General Harry Crerar, and British 2nd Army, under General Miles Dempsey-have to capture locations of strategic significance whilst simultaneously sealing up the enemy opposite sides. Meanwhile, the driving force of the 3rd American Army, obeying General George S. Patton, who directly commanded it, moving rapidly from the south, defeated heavily defended German positions and closed the potential routes of German escape. The thought of soldiers took up that all the time they must be conscious about the forthcoming encirclement was one of the circumstances, which was showing the desperate course of events.

The function of main forces at the Falaise Pocket was fundamental. The Polish 1st Armored Division, as a component of the Canadian 1st Army, was decisive in closing the gap at the point of Chambois, around which the breakthrough was made. The Polish forces were the most important ones in the pocket. They were attacked by the trapped German troops from the inside who wanted to break out, but their strict defence was crucial as in result the escape prevention and the pocket sealing were done. Also, divisions, such as the 90th Infantry and the 2nd French, made a huge contribution to the blocking of the Germans' retreats and the consolidating of the allied positions surrounding the pocket.

Intense and continuous combat marked the systematic annihilation of the trapped German forces in the Falaise Pocket. The besieged German troops were under unremitting fire from Allies' artillery, air sorties, and ground forces which functioned as a deadly vice enclosing them. Bereft of supplies and reinforcements, the Germans suffered terrible losses. The battleground turned into chaos and massacre as the Allies pushed themselves further and further, struck the German positions uncontrollably, and obviated any order in the retreat.

In the larger sense, the impact of the victory in Falaise was so serious. The elimination of the German 7th Army and the 5th Panzer Army was paid for with a large number of deaths and the wasting of crucial equipment such as tanks, artillery, and transport vehicles. The shattering of the German military power in Normandy was assured thanks to the complete defeat of the German forces. The victory at Falaise was a big blow to the German soldiers, leading to a drop in their morale, and also to the weakening of their defensive capacity in further confrontations.

The Battle of the Falaise Pocket falls under the general German resistance in Normandy, which gives the Falaise victory the credit for opening up the other two fronts. Having the Germans left hopeless, after being beaten badly, the Allies made a decision to move forward with new energy. The Paris Liberation was the next event to happen after that as the Forces of the Allies, propelled by the success they had had at Falaise, approached the French capital. The August 1944 fall of Paris was the point which makes everything else symbolic and strategic; it mobilized the strengthened efforts of the Allies and therewith, it marked a turning point in the liberation of Western Europe.

The Battle of Falaise had also a considerable impact on the general situation of the war as a whole. Thanks to the neutralization of the majority of the German military potential in the Normandy area, a shift was allowed to the further course of the campaign, more exactly to the invasion of Germany. The Germans were weakened after the Falaise disaster, which mutually facilitated the advancement of the Allies toward the German border, thus paving the way for the eventual invasion of Germany and also the final areas.

The Battle of the Falaise Pocket is without a shadow of a doubt a fight that stands out in the entire context of the Normandy campaign. The fact that Germans were encircled and killed through Allied strategy and the great cooperation among the American, British, Canadian, and Polish forces was so successful that it exemplified the idea of the Allies' measures and troops. It was a stress test of the balance and will of the soldiers of the Allies, who managed mighty obstacles to win the breakthrough needed.

Having achieved this victory, even in the past tense, as related in the immediate practical military gains became limited and this was the main point of the story. Falaise operation was meant to be a kind of a demonstration of the right way found in different situations through a combination of encirclement tactics and joint operations in modern warfare. It argued in favor, that maneuver warfare is a quintessential means of achieving success in a plethora of different scenarios, a lesson that can be learned from the Falkland case. It is again claimed that encirclement and envelopment built one of the most significant roles in the victory of Falaise. The lessons learned from Falaise influenced subsequent Allied operations, underscoring the necessity of coordination, speed, and decisive action in achieving strategic objectives.

So, in the end, the Falaise Pocket Battle was the key event in the Normandy Allied campaign. The encirclement and destruction of the German 7th Army and 5th Panzer Army marked the collapse of German resistance in the region and facilitated the rapid advance of Allied forces across France. This victory not only opened a window for the people of Paris to be free but also marked the start of the Allies going towards Germany and lastly resulting in the final victory of Europe going over the process. The heroism, tenuity, and unity displayed at Falaise are the moments that still stand out as the cornerstones of the Second World War history.

The Liberation of Paris: A Triumph of Allied Forces and French Resistance

August 1944 witnessed the freeing of Paris, a day of utmost importance not only on the military front but also as a symbol of the approaching liberation of France. At the Falaise Pocket, the Allied forces achieved a rare win, registering an irreversible success that changed the history of the campaign and the whole of Europe. France had been given back its competitive spirit. After the Falaise battle, the whole force of the Allied Army should have been sent as quickly as possible into Paris. Yet breakthroughs had to be created while controlling the territory and maintaining communication lines inside France.

Paris was a never-ending moment when the Allies commenced the attack, breaking the German army. Paris had been in a position to enable the Germans to block attacks on it due to its historic defensive position, and its location at a chokepoint within their supply lines. The elements of the German army that had been positioned between the pockets had been left isolated and as a result, the Allies were able to advance very quickly. Paris controlled not only French politics and culture but it was also a crucial link in the transportation and logistics chain. The German soldiers had to come off a chain of misinformation which would be supplied by the French. Furthermore, the low morale of the German soldiers and the resultant communication breakdown would give an advantage to the Allies and would facilitate the provision of air cover to the ground troops by their air force.

Because of the joint efforts of American, British, and Free French units, Paris was liberated. In addition to his overall leadership role, General Eisenhower also oversaw the planning and execution of a series of maneuvers that led to successful seizure of objectives instead. The Americans and the French (besides naturally courage and brilliant maneuvering) bombarded the enemies. Eventually, after an extended conversation with Major Tustin, I reached a conclusion that made me feel I wished to serve the French people not with speeches but in the fight against the Germans. Their mere courage and soldierly skills compared to the Americans' use of the latest in war technology. General Leclerc and his men who were also a part of the French 2nd Armored Division with a mission to remain on the left of the American tanks and clear the road were likewise involved in the direct fighting.

The situation with Paris was finally resolved by rapid and forceful action. With their dominant mobility and firepower, the Allied troops ignored the direct route and went around German positions through the country to the north of Paris. The invaders of the German bio-threat, facing long rows and consuming the dead uselessly with the constant pressure of the Allied offensives, were neither strong enough to mount an effective defence nor had the energy to do so. The quickness of the Allied progress made the Germans hesitate to regroup and defend Paris, moving the city into a state of higher risk for their enemies.

The thin arms of the French Resistance played a decisive role in the liberation of Paris. The movement, which was a combination of diverse groups with one common purpose, would stage sabotage attacks, as well as gather intelligence and start an uprising against the German invaders. Their successive sabotage substantially weakened German control and the prevention of which allowed the Allied to move closer to their target. The Resistance's mode of operation compromised the German supply lines, damaged communications networks, and through the use of guerrilla warfare, they caused confusion and turmoil among the occupying forces.

The cooperation between the Resistance and the Allied forces saw its best parts demonstrated in the deeds of noted generals such as General Charles de Gaulle. De Gaulle, who came into power because of the Free French Forces, became the main figure in the efforts to bring together the Resistance and make its integration into the broader Allied strategy a successful one. His leadership and insight were the driving forces that drew in the public's support for the liberation endeavours and in the end, the planning of the governing liberated France.

The fact that the liberation of Paris also has symbolic and psychological significance cannot be overstated. According to them, the people of France found in the entering of Allied forces and the liberation of the capital of their country the culmination of a period of dark occupation and the genesis of a new time of freedom and hope. It was a strong sight; the sight of Free French and Allied soldiers marching through the Champs-Élysées was cheered by celebrating Parisians at the same time. It was an image that touched every point of the world intensely.

Paris was liberated as well and this event had a truthful and great effect on the war effort that the Allies were under. The official exhibit of the victory of the Allied side and the resilience of the French people was one of the demonstrations. The harmonious interaction that was the outcome of the Resistance and the French Resistance authority demonstrated the alliance's vigour and the necessity of the local people's assistance in reaching strategic goals. The liberation of Paris, a French city, was not only of great importance to the Allied morale but also acted as an important sign for the babe to tell that, indeed, the war was umbrageously shifting away from the Axis powers.

During Allies' occupation of Paris, Germans also protested the incursion but it was eventually subdued. The German garrison that General Dietrich von Choltitz led finally surrendered on 25th August 1944. This happened after impassioned plea from both the Resistance and the advancing Allied troops. The surrender was the final act that ended the totalitarian occupation of the German army squad and this also became a heralding of the end of German superintendence in France.

The liberation of Paris had a direct effect that spread over a long time on the Allied operation. It initially became a point of convergence for the coordination of operations with the transportation hub at the forefront which expedited the Allies' successful attempt in moving close to the German border. The city was the centre for further planning and execution in Western Europe. Again, in the long run, the liberation of Paris gave the Allied troops a moral advantage over the Axis forces and also served as the initiation electromotive that attracted the other resistance movements peppered all across the occupied Europe.

The rest of the Allies was in Paris and the disagreement in the group never rose to the surface. The successful incorporation of the Free French military units into the Allied chain of command and the collaboration with the Resistance set off a clear proof of the robustness and resoluteness of the alliance in the liberation of Europe. The togetherness would prove essential in the final stages of the war in the days and weeks when the Allies moved into Germany and the final defeat of the Nazi regime was the only option remaining.

There can be no doubt that the liberation of Paris was a record accomplishment in Europe. The planned movement and the ultimate actions of the Alliance were in the right direction of reaching their goal in such a way as the war was a fight beyond the immediate battlefield. Paris was not only liberated-over of occupation by the Germans, it also represented freedom to the whole of France and the failure of the Nazi regime in winning over Europe.

Across the Fields of Liberation: Allied Advances Through France

The successful trip all around France, which took place after the Paris was liberated, the sweep of area battles and the entrance of the regions, was crucially done, giving way for the total collapse of Western European German defense. The brilliant strategies of the commanders, the fact that the soldiers kept going on their mission and the support given to them by the local resistance all were the main reasons for the very tough campaign.

The bold advance of the Allies went on with great determination after Paris fell down till the substantial territories and cities of France were put in the free bandwagon. One of the most iconic battles is the Battle of the Bulge, which occurred in December 1944 to January 1945. This was considered as the last major German attack on the Western Front, which aimed at both the division of the Allies and the taking of the West coast of Belgium- the critical seaport of Antwerp. The greatest achievement in this battle was mainly the war competition in Ardennes forest with major participants including American forces, which notably made a name for themselves through a variety of activities, such as resistance and taking of Bastogne, which were being surrounded and outgunned. General George S. Patton's 3rd Army contribution was so impactful, as they did not only rescue the besieged troops but also switched the control of power in favor of the Allies, thereby leading to the Allies' final victory.

The release of cities as big as Lyon and Strasbourg represented the main stages in the attempt for the Allies. Lyon was one of the key sources of the war machine and the logistics center which was released by General Jean de Lattre de Tassigny with the help of the Free French Forces in September 1944. This was not only the break in the German supply lines, but also, it was another morale booster for the French in addition to the resistance movements. Strasbourg, which had great symbolic significance, was freed in November 1944 by the French 2nd Armored Division that was under General Philippe Leclerc's leadership. The lastly mentioned event led to the final assertion of the Allied dominion in Eastern France, and the invasion of the German territory.

The conquest by the allied army of the French countryside was the occasion of a great many battles and the steady emancipation of occupied towns and villages. Forces of the United States, Great Britain, Canada, and Free France displayed the highest point of cooperation and agility in the face of strong German opposition. Strategic leaders such as General Dwight D. Eisenhower, Field Marshal Bernard Montgomery, and General Omar Bradley masterminded the plans and stuck to it, which included ground attacks, air support, and logistical planning. Operations to recover French cities such as Marseille and Toulon, in the south of the country, through Operation Dragoon, symbolized the tactical planning of naval and ground units, which imprisoned the Germans in the north and liberated the Mediterranean coastline.

It is true that the failure of the German defense activities in France was the result of various interconnected causes. Continuous fighting by the Allies during summer and autumn of 1944 greatly reduced the number of German soldiers and resources. The Allies' harassing tactics in combination with their numerical superiority and superior fire put the Germans in a weak position preventing them from organizing counterattacks. The strategic bombings planned by the Allies involved in the destruction of German supply lines and their communication. These bombings affected the main structural such as railways, bridges, and factories, thus, the German army suffered great losses and was no longer able to send more soldiers as well as their front-line units did not have more supplies.

The weakening of the German military due to which the men became below the strength of the units that were previously incapacitated by the attack and the frequent rates of casualty were the contributing factors. The German General Staff had a hard time replacing soldiers and equipment that were lost and as a result, there was a slow but there might be an unchangeable weakening of their defense. The use of young and elderly men as well as foreign conscripts was not the exact state of the German powers. Furthermore, the disastrous effect of the continuous thrashing and withdrawal on the German moral and combat effectiveness was further intensified by the psychological implications.

Unification of the Allied forces in multiple countries was crucial in achieving these successes. The fusion of armed forces from various countries into a coherent powerful arsenal certainly showcased the unity of the Allied coalition. The United States, in their capacity to draw on vast resources and their logistics, played a most significant role in keeping the developments going. The British and Canadian units showed their experience and tactical expertise, and the Free French Forces gave invaluable local information and support, which made the whole of the Allied campaign all the more effective.

The constant pressure on the fugitive German forces was of great strategic significance. The Allies pursued an unending offensive, which refused any chance to the Germans to get together again and adopt a new defense policy. The fast and continual moving in on the German border enabled the adversary to adapt, build, and successfully kill the Allied advancements, but the pace of the war never allowed that. By steadfastly maintaining pressure on the enemy and capturing every opportunity, the Allies progressively achieved the success they did in France.

The situation was followed by the release of France making a significant impact in the overall war effort. The capture deprived the Germans of a large piece of land, and in addition, the Allies obtained the vital area that was to be used as a launch pad for the final push into Germany. The liberation of French ports and transportation networks and the industrial centers of France gained important logistical and strategic advantages as well.

Also, a fully independent France under the control of the Free French government under Charles de Gaulle brought military and political motivations to the significant increase of the Allied side.

Moreover, the liberation of France was such a powerful and moral effect on the Allied forces and the citizens of France. The cities have been found in gory details, returned refugees, and France found herself to newly, and freely be a democratic and revitalized country which has restored a spirit of resistance and determination to achieve the ultimate goal. This raised the resurgence of a new sense of purpose and unity which was key to the Allied Force winning the war. They turned their attention to the invasion and liberation of Germany, which was the last and most difficult part of the war with a sense of a common purpose.

On the other hand, the advance of the Allies in France involved large battles, tactical victories, and the weakening of the defences of the Germans. The simultaneous efforts of the multinational Allied Forces as well as the continued assaults and strategic bombing campaigns contributed to the liberation of the major cities and regions. The defeat of the German forces in France eventually cleared the way for the aggressive push through Germany and hence the decisive turning point of the Second World War and the subsequent winning of the Allies in Europe.

Sustaining Victory: The Logistical and Strategic Challenges of the Allied Advance

When the Allies moved over France after the Normandy invasion, they confronted a couple of different problems, both logistical and strategic, which they feared would impair their advancement. The problems that companies might confront when they want to suffice the demand of the top customers and get rid of unproductive elements in logistics are in fact, hundreds to count. The need of a steady flow of reinforcements, the establishment of supply lines, and the conducting of the whole logistic operation under the premium quality were some of the most innovative ways to solve these problems. The given part talks about how essential the vicissitude of the everyday situations was when it came to allied success in the battlefield and they moreover needed to come through certain formidable difficulties.

The speedy march of the allies through France needed them to establish and protect the very increasing substantial supplies chains. As multiple were moving away from the Normandy beachheads the logistical needs made a great leap ahead. The necessity to arm the, the front-line unit, with ammunition, fuel, food, and medical supplies was a relic means of increasing the speed of the next attack. One of the biggest logistical challenges was that the supplies were to be moved over the great distance and often through the territories inhibited by either the adversaries or damaged infrastructure as the case of the newly liberated area.

In order to meet these difficulties, the Allies initiated some smart strategies of action. One of the most remarkable was, for example, the building of special ports, e.g. Mulberry Harbours, at Gold Beach and Omaha Beach. These makeshift harbours allowed the quick offloading of goods right from the ships, tip-toeing around the shipping of the goods to bases that were under the protective wing of the Germans or the ones that were severely smashed. The Mulberry harbours were a kind of new structures that the allies had built and that helped them a lot to support their operations during the early stages of their advance greatly.

With the gradual extension of the front lines to the farther-inland areas, air supply drops became a vital part of the logistics strategy. To some extent, the use of aircraft as a means of direct supply delivery to the front-line units was successful in removing the vulnerabilities and delays encountered with ground transport. These air drops were of tremendous importance to the fighters in the most critical battles because not only did they shield them but also fed them with whatever was necessary to push them forward. The air supply missions flexibility supported by quickness was, in essence, the cornerstone of the Allies' thrilling movement across France.

A further solution to logistical problems that was implemented most effectively included running the Red Ball Express convoy system. The network was operated by a large number of truck convoys that operated all day and night between the Normandy beachheads and the advancing front lines. The Red Ball Express was made up mainly by African American soldiers who, by assisting in the supply of the supplies, played a major part in the success of the operation. The transport system was an outstanding example of the logistics ingenuity and resolve of the Allied forces, which was a way to overcome the major transportation problems and continuing of the offensive operations.

The absolute necessity of getting and using ports, railways, and roads to the carrying out of advance operations is a fact that needs to be emphasized. Ports such as Cherbourg, and later Antwerp also became crucial to the logistical plans of the Allies once they were conquered and fixed. These ports allowed for the transportation of massive numbers of supplies and equipment, that were then remitted to the front-line units. The acquisition and restoration of main rails and road networks were also of key importance for swift resource movement. The recovery of infrastructure by retreating German forces and Allied bombardment missions resulted in tough difficulties, managers spent a lot of their work repairing and rebuilding transportation networks.

Our ability to easily manage all the logistical requirements was due to the collaboration of the soldiers from various Allied nations and different military branches. The formation of the Supreme Headquarters Allied Expeditionary Force (SHAEF) with General Dwight D. Eisenhower as its head was a single control structure that led to joint cooperation. The regular exchange of information and holding of dietary and blood pressure readings ensured that the logistic ports were selected according to tactical plans, facilitating an increase in resources and their optimized use.

The purposeful destruction of infrastructure by the withdrawing German forces was the technique used to prohibit the Allies advance. The primary target of such actions were bridges, railways, and roads that were always repair conditions to the Allies' fleet. To meet the shortage in the military forces and be able to operate uphill the Allies had to mend and rebuild infrastructure. Despite the availability of first-welded units for the Allied forces, they actually made necessary efforts to solve the transport problem- thus supply routes continued to be available. Weer the employment of Bailey bridges became the replacement of the demolished river crossings and was the best way to ensure the flow of goods would not be stopped by the invaders.

The critical role of logistics to the success of the Allied campaign was indeed vital. The visibility of which conditions were easily and at the same time continuously met was the only guarantee of not only the next major supply and the cohesively managed personnel as well. The crucial operation of sending more soldiers to battle and sending damaged vehicles to be repaired and replaced is the logistic department that was non-transferable among them. The whole logistic apparatus developed by the Allies was a remarkable achievement of both their world view and their functional flexibility.

Among the branches of the military, the army, navy, and air force played a significant role in the effective handling of logistical challenges. The navy, for instance, was instrumental in providing safe sea routes and directing cargoes to port destinations while the air force contributed by carrying out important air support and supply drop-offs. The combined operation of these branches made sure that the supply chains were well managed and that they responded on time to the frontline units.

An additional strategic necessity was to ensure the continuous pursuit of the retreating German armed forces. The Allies found no time to relax or regroup, and all their actions were directed at the enemy, not giving them a break to make new defensive lines. The high-speed and the continuous movement towards the German border resulted in the enemy always being caught off-guard, which led to them not reinforcing important positions and effectively resisting the advancing Allies. The tactics which include enduring pressure and seizing on any break in the enemy's lines programmed by the Allies in the campaign of France.

In a nutshell, it was no small challenge that the Allies faced not only on the strategic but also the logistical aspects during their transformative campaign in France. The ability to keep the supply lines flowing, the proper shipment of reinforcements, and the organization of the hugest logistic operations demanded innovative ways backed up by well-timed coordination. The use of portable ports, air supply drops, and the Red Ball Express convoy system represented the logistical creativity of the Allies. The eponymous the Midway movie depicting the Allies universes in the period of World War II was the relationship of the accord between Allied nations and the rest of the branches of the military with the pressing on the retreating forces of Germany that ensured the success of the campaign and the liberation of the European countries that would finally take place. The skirmishes of these soldiers who were sometimes retarding but also capable resulted from the preparedness to fall back on them when solving logistic snags, their competitiveness (as the) imbuing them with the ability to win their way through other threats as they headed to Germany.

The Final Thrust: Allies' Road to Germany

The task of the Allies in France really was the continuation of the integrity and honor of the whole project whose aiming was the final passage into Germany without whose success the outcome of World War II would have been completely different escalating drastically without stopping. This was the one great work of the sort that the war would leave surviving the careful planning of the military with resulting the distribution of all the resources and the coordination of the international army. The development of intelligence and the employment of reconnaissance were the essential components with regard to the final offensive strategies.

A strategy of an attack on Germany was composed of planning at different levels that involved every key figure. Top-ranking authorities led by General Dwight D. Eisenhower and his Supreme Headquarters Allied Expeditionary Force (SHAEF) were outstanding in stimulating American, British, Canadian, and French troops. The prioritization of the massive destruction of the Nazi menace was the first phase of the master plan followed by the strategic assault on Germany.

Not allowing any kind of the German forces along the western border of Germany would be out of reach for the United States. The Siegfried Line, a complex of bulwarks spread from west to east along the German border, made the first line of defense against the Allies. The awareness among the Allies that the line was the paramount barrier that could only be broken if they pulled everything together and possessed the right amount of fire was realized. The opening attacks dealt with capturing the most strategic towns and cities that would establish as the launching points. Aachen, the first German city that surrendered to the Allies was a key victory that allowed them to get to the core of Germany and was ammunition for German morale.

Intelligence and reconnaissance were the main forces in the determination of the final offensive strategies. The British MI6 and American OSS, the intelligence agencies of the Allies, operated day and night to acquire data such as German troop locations, fortifications, and supply lines. Spyplanes that moved through the air and land-based reconnaisance were the main way for them to get access to the strategic disposition of the enemy. With the help of this intelligence, Allied planners could be able to figure out natural weak points in the Sigfried Line giving them the idea how to make the stronghold fail or other strategies engineers might have for dismantling it.

The resources were allocated to the final stage making it another most important part of these preparations project. The Allies assembled a large amount of supplies, equipment, and personnel for the final offensive. The problems of logistics were very challenging, as the network of transportation, supply depots, and field hospitals had to be coordinated. By a good management of the resources these units were always well -equipped and they could sustain a prolonged offensive. The usage of temporary bridges, repairing of damaged structures, occupying the forward operational zones made a quick relocation of personnel and matériel possible.

The communication of the forces of different countries became a factor in the success of the last attack. There were strong planning and communication required for the establishment of the integrated US, British, Canadian, and French bodies into the single fighting force. Joint operations, the ones that were linked to the Battle of the Bulge, brought out the most remarkable outcomes demonstrated by the Allies working together. The willingness to integrate different troops and utilize their specific abilities was the proof of the fact that the Allies had the resolution to act unitedly, which they deserved to be congratulated for.

The change of France's fate and the penetration of the Allies into Germany in the future has many long-term impacts. The successful Allied campaign was important not only in finishing the war but also in laying the structure for the new Europe after World War II. The political and social significance of the liberation process was so wide-reaching that the occupied countries were able to recover their independence and start the process of rehabilitation.

The liberation of France was a finally reached the point where the German control of the territory was weakened and the opposition was united across the whole area. The Nazi occupation's collapse in France had been the catalyst for revolts in other lands occupied by German forces, eventually depriving the latter of international recognition. The comeback of the French state under the leadership of General Charles de Gaulle was seen as an example of successful administration after war and the development of democratic institutions was likewise proven.

The later Allied advance to Germany was, in a pivotal manner, the determining factor in the overall outcome of the war. This unrelenting resulting in the Germans concentrating their energy eastwards thus weakening their resistance to the Soviet onslaught as the Allies applied continuous pressure. The occupation of crucial industrial centers, such as the Ruhr Valley, paralysed the German maneuvers in the war and sped up the collapse of the Third Reich.

The political and social ramification of the liberation of France and the consequent Allied penetration of Germany went far beyond the initial battlefield victories. The contention between the Allies and the liberated territories laid the path for post-war reconstruction and durability. The Allies executed measures that would bring back sanity, reconstruct the collapsed infrastructure, and ease the recovery of war-torn economies.

The Marshall Plan which was started after the war gave a shot in the arm to the European economies and politician.

The Freedom of France and the following Allied domination played a decisive role in the formation of the post-World War geopolitics. The allotment of Germany into occupation zones, which were agreed on the Yalta and Potsdam Conferences, actually depicted the strategic advantages of the Allied powers and provided the basis for a Cold-War stage. On the one hand, Western Europe was occupied by the USA, and its allies which were generally democratic while Soviet-controlled the other parts of Europe so these differences led to disunity in Europe which resulted in a divided Europe.

These events had not only a short but also a long-term influence on the Europe after the World War II which is really one of those events that was marked by a large phase change. The movement of the Western Front to other places was a turning point in the war.

The new world order was first born out of Allied victory in WWII. The principles of democracy, self-determination, and collective security, enshrined in institutions such as the United Nations and NATO, were bolstered by the war events. The reconstruction of Europe and the establishment of the new, stable, and prosperous post-war order were without any doubt the direct result of the Allied forces' sacrifice and success.

In short, the way to Germany was full of detailed arrangements, strategic design, and multinational powers' massive coordination. The saving of France and the advance of Allies into Germany which followed had a very significant overall effect on the result of the war and the subsequent order of Europe. The effective adaptation of secret service, logistics, and military operations was the reason why the walls of German defense had collapsed and hence provided a favorable situation for the final victory of the Allies. The long lasting outcomes from these events still show how the geopolitical landscape has been shaped at that time, which underscores the importance of the Allies' activities in the Second World War.

Appendix

Key Commanders in the Allied Advance Across France and Into Germany

General Dwight D. Eisenhower

As the Supreme Commander of the Allied Expeditionary Force, General Dwight D. Eisenhower played a pivotal role in the strategic planning and execution of the Normandy invasion and the subsequent Allied advance across France and into Germany. His leadership was instrumental in coordinating the efforts of the multi-national Allied forces, ensuring seamless integration and effective collaboration among American, British, Canadian, and French troops. Eisenhower's ability to maintain unity and focus among diverse military branches was critical to the success of the campaign.

Field Marshal Bernard Montgomery

Field Marshal Bernard Montgomery commanded the British 21st Army Group, which included British and Canadian forces. Known for his meticulous planning and caution, Montgomery led the forces during the critical phases of the Normandy invasion and the Battle of Normandy. He played a significant role in the liberation of Caen and the subsequent breakout operations. Montgomery's leadership was crucial in maintaining pressure on German forces and facilitating the coordinated advances that led to the capture of key strategic positions.

General Omar Bradley

General Omar Bradley commanded the American 12th Army Group, which included the First and Third U.S. Armies. Bradley's leadership was vital during the breakout from Normandy, particularly in Operation Cobra, which led to the encirclement of German forces at the Falaise Pocket. His strategic acumen ensured the rapid advance of American forces across France, contributing significantly to the liberation of key cities and the eventual push into Germany.

General George S. Patton

General George S. Patton, known for his aggressive tactics and rapid maneuvers, commanded the U.S. Third Army. Patton's leadership was instrumental in the breakout from Normandy and the subsequent rapid advance across France. His bold and decisive actions during the Battle of the Bulge were critical in relieving the besieged town of Bastogne. Patton's ability to exploit weaknesses in German defences and maintain momentum was a key factor in the Allied success.

General Charles de Gaulle

General Charles de Gaulle, leader of the Free French Forces, played a crucial role in both the military and political arenas. His leadership was instrumental in coordinating French resistance efforts and integrating them with Allied operations. De Gaulle's presence during the liberation of Paris was symbolic of the restoration of French sovereignty. His efforts helped to unify French resistance movements and ensure their significant contribution to the Allied war effort.

General Harry Crerar

General Harry Crerar commanded the First Canadian Army, which played a vital role in the Battle of Normandy and the subsequent liberation of northern France and the Low Countries.

Crerar's leadership was crucial in securing key positions and maintaining the momentum of the Allied advance. His forces were instrumental in closing the Falaise Pocket and advancing into the Netherlands.

General Philippe Leclerc

General Philippe Leclerc, commander of the French 2nd Armoured Division, was a key figure in the liberation of Paris. His division was among the first Allied units to enter the French capital, and his leadership during the drive towards Strasbourg and other key objectives in eastern France was pivotal. Leclerc's actions were emblematic of the French contribution to the Allied victory and the restoration of French national pride.

These commanders, through their strategic brilliance, tactical acumen, and inspirational leadership, were instrumental in the Allied campaign across France and into Germany. Their achievements not only facilitated military victories but also laid the foundations for the post-war reconstruction and stability of Europe.